Every M

Every Man

~by~

Daniel Henley

Every Woman,
Every Man

~by~

Daniel Henley

Living Word Books

Cordova, Tennessee

Some scripture (indicated NIV) taken from the HOLY BIBLE, NEW INTERNATIONAL VERSION®. Copyright © 1973, 1978, 1984 International Bible Society. Used by permission of Zondervan. All rights reserved. The "NIV" and "New International Version" trademarks are registered in the United States Patent and Trademark Office by International Bible Society. Use of either trademark requires the permission of International Bible Society.

Some scripture (indicated NRSV) taken from the New Revised Standard Version Bible, copyright 1989, Division of Christian Education of the National Council of the Churches of Christ in the United States of America. Used by permission. All rights reserved.

Some scripture taken from *The Message*. Copyright © 1993, 1994, 1995, 1996, 2000, 2001, 2002. Used by permission of NavPress Publishing Group.

Some Scripture quotations (indicated AMP) taken from the Amplified® Bible, Copyright © 1954, 1958, 1962, 1964, 1965, 1987 by The Lockman Foundation. Used by permission." (www.Lockman.org)

Some scripture (indicated KJV) take from the King James Version of the Holy Bible.

ISBN: 978-0-9819261-6-2

Library of Congress Control Number: 2010922237

Living Word Books
Double-Edged Publishing, Inc.
9618 Misty Brook Cove
Cordova, Tennessee 38016

For the word of God is living and active. Sharper than any double-edged sword, it penetrates even to dividing soul and spirit, joints and marrow; it judges the thoughts and attitudes of the heart.
Hebrews 4:12 New International Version (NIV)

www.doubleedgedpublishing.com

Printed in the United States of America

First Printing

Dedication

Father God, we dedicate this book to you. May it bring you glory, honor and praise. We love you Lord.

What Every Woman Needs to Hear, What Every Man Needs to Know

Introduction	1

Part One

I Give What I Want	5
Sharing God's Forgiveness	15
Tradition	25
Purpose	37
Balance In ALL Things	45

Part Two

Doing Your Part	61
It's A Matter of Life & Death	73
Defending Against "The Threat"	81
Living in "The Blessing"	97
A Final Prayer	107

Acknowledgements

This project would not have been possible without a lot of folks. Just to name a few. Thanks to our editing team of Karen Henley, Dee Henley, James Henley, Memphis Jones, Audrey Bullock and Takasha Neil. I would also like to acknowledge my accountability partners and friends, Travis Moody and Pastor Dana Keye. Without your love, support and prayers, this would have never happened. Thanks to my parents, James and Mary Henley, who always seem to send a check in the mail at the exact time it is needed. We love you and thank you so much. Thanks also to our leadership team at Journey Christian Church; because you do what you do so well, it frees me up to do what I do. And lastly, but definitely not least, to my Queen, Dee Henley; I love you dearly!

Every Woman, Every Man

~by~

Daniel Henley

Introduction

Little Daniel, our son who was eight years old at the time, was playing a game where he would hide under the blankets of our bed and ask me the question, "Can you see me?" I answered him and said, "Yes, you are under the blanket." However, I never looked up from what I was doing. We repeated this process several times with Daniel asking me over and over again, "Can you see me?" Finally Daniel loudly proclaimed, "You can't see me because you are doing your work."

At that time I looked up and could see he was peeping out from under the blanket and that he could see me. Daniel knew there was no way that I could have seen him because my eyes were focused on what I was doing the whole time we were playing the game. It wasn't until I stopped my will, which was to do my work that I could actually see my precious little boy peeping out from under the blanket. He asked me again, "Can you see me?"

This time when I said, "Yes, you are under the blanket," I was actually looking at him peeping from under the blanket. He knew for the first time I could see him. We repeated this process several times and little Daniel laughed so hard that you would have thought I was tickling him. We both enjoyed his simple little game of... "Can you see me?"

> *While seeing they don't see, and while*
> *hearing they don't hear; otherwise*
> *they might turn and be forgiven.*
> *-Mark 4:12*

So many times, right-relationships between a woman and a man boil down to this one issue. Can you see me? Can you see beyond the surface and identify my inward needs? Can you see behind the words to hear the voice behind the voice crying out for help? Can you see the pain or the anger lurking beneath the surface just waiting to explode? Can you see the hopes and the dreams or the uncertainties and the fears?

This book is intended to glorify God by helping to empower right-relationships to be all that God purposed them to be. Not only will it help us to see more clearly, but it will also teach us how to apply some very powerful principles that will help guide any relationship.

In this book you will learn The Four Laws of Covenant Relationships. The Four Laws of Covenant Relationship are based on principles that have been established by God. They work the same way all the time whether we realize they are working or not. They work the same for the Christian and the non-Christian. They work the same for the saved person as they do for the lost. In Genesis 8:22 we read:

As long as the earth endures, seedtime and harvest, cold and heat, summer and winter, day and night will never cease.

An example of an established principle that is always in operation is The Law of Seedtime and Harvest. The Law of Seedtime and Harvest states that if you plant during seedtime you will have an opportunity for a harvest. If you never participate in seedtime, you will never have a harvest. You can pray for a harvest, cry and wail for a harvest or even try to scheme and manipulate for a harvest, but you will never produce a harvest unless you planted during seedtime. The Law of Seedtime and Harvest is an established principle by God. It works the same way, all the time.

Likewise, the Law of Gravity is an established principle by God that works the same way, all the time. If you climb up on top of a ten story building and jump off, the law of gravity says you will hit the ground. Whatever goes up must eventually come down. The Law of Gravity was in operation before you decided to jump off the building. You simple proved it to yourself when you tried it.

The Four Laws of Covenant Relationship work in the same way. The laws are established principles by God which are in operation at all times, whether we are working them or not. The Four Laws of Covenant Relationship are:

1. Each party is responsible to do what is good for the covenant relationship.
2. To keep the covenant agreement is rewardable by entering into the Life Cycle; and to break the covenant agreement is punishable by entering into the Death Cycle.

3. When we do our part in the covenant relationship, we defend against "the threat."
4. God honors and blesses those who honor and bless the covenant relationship.

Before we can truly apply these very powerful yet practical laws to our relationships, it is imperative that we spend a little time understanding both the challenges and opportunities that most relationships face. In what you're about to read, you will meet a lot of people. All of the folks that we refer to in this book are real. There are no character actors and this is not make believe. We have changed all of the names and some of the situations slightly in order to maintain the integrity of what we do, but we want you to know the people are real - just like you. God sees you and He knows your situation. May this book be a blessing to all who read it and hear the message.

-1-

I Give What I Want

"Pressure induces a response from people" "Faith induces a response from God"

It was day one of my sabbatical. I had just announced to our congregation the prior Sunday that I would take a month off to seek God for direction for our church. Just in case you don't know, a sabbatical is just a long vacation with the intent of resting, relaxing and receiving insight and direction from God. It's a time to get away from it all and just hear from God. Moses went up to the mountain for forty days and came back with the Ten Commandments. Jesus went into the desert for forty days and came back to start His ministry. While I wasn't able to sign up for forty days, I was able to take thirty days and WOW, what a time with God.

What is interesting is that on the very first day, I had a late evening conversation with a dear family member who I'll just call Heather for the purposes of this writing. My family is very close and we usually talk quite often; however, Heather and I had not had an extended conversation for some time. We had the "how are you and the family?" talks that lasted all of about three minutes, but nothing like the nights we use to have where we would talk for hours. This would be one of those nights.

We spoke about many things and eventually I told Heather I was writing another book while on sabbatical. I asked her for her thoughts about what I could do better or differently this time around. You see, we had written our first book, Empowering Right Relationships, with a team of Spirit Writers. A Spirit Writer is someone that would listen to audio recordings of certain teachings that I had done and then they would turn that into written form.

While we were truly successful, this time around I was committed to doing the hard work of writing the book myself.

Heather suggested I write a "feel good" book. She said that most people just want to feel good and sometimes a book can be the instrument. She went on to give me several examples of some "feel good" stories.

The first story she shared with me was about a single mom she had seen on the Oprah Winfrey show. The mom had pulled herself out from a horrible situation. Her husband had committed suicide and about three months prior to that he had stopped paying all the bills. She was in a situation where she had no money, no insurance, all her bills were past due and she hadn't worked in over ten years. After seeking some good advice, she reached out to her closet relatives and friends and asked how they could help her out.

One relative said that they could watch the kids while she looked for a job. Another said they could give her a $1,000 per month until she could get back on her feet and the list went on and on. The point of this "feel good" story was that sometimes we just have to reach out to others and let them know our situation and we are in need of help. Instead of waiting for them to offer, we should just ask them, "How can you help?" It was truly a "feel good" story with a very happy ending. The lady did get back on her feet; got a good job and both she and her children are prospering.

The second story she shared with me was a similar kind of "feel good" story and it too had a happy ending. However, it was the third story that she shared with me that really caught my attention. It didn't fit into the same mode of the previous two stories. It almost seemed out of place. And it definitely wasn't a "feel good" story.

In the third story that Heather shared with me, she told me about a lady whose husband had built her a $300,000 house, sold it for $700,000 and they now lived in a 1.3 million dollar house. She went on to say the lady told her she had gone to church on one particular Sunday and the preacher said the church needed money. She politely gave them $100; which was quite a bit for her, since she normally would only give five or ten dollars each Sunday.

Heather said she was shocked because she was thinking to herself that this lady lives in a 1.3 million dollar home and she normally gives the church five or ten dollars a week. Not being able to contain herself, she said to the lady, "I can't believe that you only give such a small amount to your church. I grew up giving ten percent of everything that I earn to the church." The lady looked at Heather in complete amazement and said, "I have never even thought about giving ten percent of what I earn. I have never even heard of such a thing."

Heather went on to say, as she was continuing to tell me that story, "that's why I left my last church." She said, every time the pastor would get up to ask for the offering, he would encourage the people to give in two envelopes. The white envelope was for the church and the purple envelope was for the pastor and his family. You see, the pastor didn't take a salary and the way he and his family were compensated was by the giving that came in the purple envelopes. Heather then said these words, "I think the pastor should take a salary and I don't need a man to get up every Sunday and tell me what to give…. **I give what I want.**"

I Give What I Want

Those five words, "**I give what I want**," have intrigued me to no end. I have been meditating on those very words every since that conversation. Why? Because after being married for over twenty-five years and having been a relationship counselor to thousands of people, I can honestly say that herein we find the answer to most of the relationship problems that people face.

First of all, what happened to the "feel good" stories? They were replaced with what was really on Heather's heart. While Heather was advising me to give "feel good" stories in my new book, seemingly out of the blue, she slipped into a story that had no particular significance to what we were discussing. The personal story about why she had left her last church came from seemingly out of nowhere; or did it?

The bible says that out of the abundance of the heart the mouth speaks. If you keep listening to people long enough they will tell you exactly what's on their heart. An unknown philosopher once said it this way, "one of the deepest desires of the human soul is to know that you've been heard." People want to be heard! Not just listened to, but heard.

One of the most important things we do as relationship counselors is to teach people how to listen. To listen in such a way as to truly hear what the other person is saying. We must learn how to stop all the chatter that goes on in our head; mostly about what we want to say next, and truly listen. Listen for understanding and not to criticize. Listen in such a way that even if you don't get another word in, your partner knows that they've been heard. You will be amazed at the results!

Secondly, what Heather was saying about her giving, "I give what they want", is exactly what most folks do in relationships; they give what they want. But in essence they give what they want...to give. In other words, she was saying that she will give what she wants to give and no one is going to influence that. However, in relationships, what we have found is it's only when we change our thinking and change that statement ever so slightly that we find the joy, contentment and peace in relationships that we seek. *I give what I want... to receive!*

Below are some very powerful words to live by:

> Give, and it will be given to you. A good measure, pressed down, shaken together and running over, will be poured into your lap. For with the measure you use (give), it will be measured (given) to you
> - Luke 6:38

> Do not be deceived: God cannot be mocked. A man reaps what he sows
> - Galatians 6:7

> Let us not become weary in doing good, for at the proper time we will reap a harvest if we do not give up
> - Galatians 6:9

> As long as the earth endures,
> seedtime and harvest, cold and heat,
> summer and winter, day and night
> will never cease
> - Genesis 8:22

Remember this: Whoever sows sparingly will also reap sparingly, and whoever sows generously will also reap generously. Everyone should give what they have decided in their heart to give, not reluctantly or under compulsion, for God loves a cheerful giver
-   2 Corinthians 9:6-7

For God so loved the world that he gave his one and only Son, that whoever believes in him shall not perish but have eternal life
-   John 3:16

Note: God gave (sowed) a son and He reaped a harvest of sons and daughters. God gave what he wanted to receive!

I believe that if I were only allowed to teach one principle to married couples, other than the importance of their individual relationships with God, this would be it. Give to your spouse, what you want to receive from them. If you want love; give love. If you want a friend; be a friend. If you want forgiveness… forgive.

Recently Dee and I were teaching a marriage enrichment seminar and we were going through an exercise on how to resolve disagreements. As with most of our seminars, we were dealing with a real life situation and a current issue that we were having in our own marriage. That's right! After twenty-five years of marriage and after counseling thousands of others, we still have issues. However, to my surprise, on this particular night, the issue my wife decided to deal with was her issue with time management.

Dee had always had a habit of being very carefree and she was notorious for being late. It was as if, we had given up hope she would ever change. We simply made accommodations to allow for her being late. However, for some odd reason, on this particular night she wanted to apply one of the tools that we use for resolving disagreements to her time issues.

The process goes like this; there are seven steps that we use for resolving disagreements.

The Seven Steps to Resolving Disagreements

1. Pray a simple unity prayer of agreement asking God to help you resolve your differences. After praying together as a couple, schedule a convenient time and place to discuss the issue at hand.

2. Define the one issue that you will be discussing. It is important to know what issue you are working on and agree to focus on that issue only. Remember, you can resolve other issues on another occasion. Stay focused on the issue at hand.

3. Brainstorm: write down as many creative ideas as you can think of that might resolve the issue. Remember there are no bad ideas. Everything goes on the list for discussion

4. Discuss each alternative solution and after reviewing the advantages and disadvantages for each, pick one idea to try. It is important here to be specific about what each of you will do to help resolve the issue.

5. Schedule another convenient time and place for your next meeting to review your progress.

6. Celebrate small victories along the way. Try to catch each other doing something right and celebrate any little progress you're making towards your goal. Celebrate early and celebrate often!

7. If the issue persists, pray and fast together for a period of time. Fasting is just the abstinence from food and it allows us to hear clearly from God. If after that, you are still unable to resolve your conflict, please seek wise Godly counsel.

For reasons known only to Dee at the time, she wanted to resolve an issue we had been dealing with in our marriage for over twenty years. We had tried many different approaches to resolving the issue of her time management. We had tried everything from day planners to me becoming Dee's personal secretary reminding her of her upcoming task and obligations. While we had seen a few glimpses of success from time to time; nothing seemed to work permanently. It seemed as though we were constantly coming back to this same issue over and over again.

However, something seemed to be different this time. For the first time, I wasn't pushing it. Dee actually recommended we tackle the issue of her time management. As we worked through the seven steps to resolving disagreements, there was a marked difference in the tone of our conversation. Instead of me coming up with the ideas, it seemed as if Dee was taking the initiative and actually leading the discussion. It was as if for the first time in over twenty years, she wanted to do better with her time management. Why now? What had changed?

It didn't dawn on me what had happened until I heard one of our newlywed couples, who were participating in that seminar give their report on the issue they were dealing with and the one solution they had agreed to try.

The couple had been married less than a year and they were going through the normal first year newlywed "stuff." They had identified that their biggest problem was - selfishness. They had the "what about me?" syndrome.

In order to resolve their issue with selfishness, they agreed to find at least five things everyday to do for each other. In other words, whatever they wanted to receive from their partner, they decided to give to their partner. I give what I want... to receive!

Then it hit me! That's exactly what I had done in our relationship. Although I hadn't told Dee until that very night, a year or so prior to that night I had decided that I would not hassle Dee any longer about her issue with time management. Instead I would do any and everything I could to help her. And I would help her without expecting or needing to receive any gratitude. I resolved in my mind that I would help her because I loved her and because she is the best thing on this earth to ever happen to me.

I started by adding Dee to my calendar at work. I would have my meetings on one side of my calendar and Dee's on the other side. I reminded her of important tasks she needed to be aware of. I would check email for her and also her voicemail, since we shared a cell phone at the time. I would then write down the important task for her. I would remind her of everything from doctor's appointments to choir rehearsal and even the days she was scheduled to work as a part-time nurse at the clinic. I would do all this without giving in to my personal desire to let her know all I was doing for her. I wanted for us as a couple to be more time sensitive and manage our time better, so I decided to give to Dee what I wanted... to receive!

I had been doing this for so long that I had forgotten I was doing it. It had been well over a year when suddenly on this one night, seemingly out of the blue, Dee decides to tackle this issue. We came up with a very simple plan of which Dee has taken ownership. Basically all we did was put a large calendar on a wall in one of our hallways and we write down anything important for Dee to do.

Our whole family has gotten involved and even our teen-age girls are excited to see how the plan is working. The whole family is having a wonderful time helping mom, by writing things down and Dee loves that her time is being better utilized. She finds she is not as anxious as she used to be because she is not always running late. She is more organized with her time and she loves it! The plan is currently paying big dividends in our marriage both now and I believe for many years to come. But what was the key? What encouraged her to take the bull by the horn and deal with it? I believe with everything in me that the key was very simple, I gave what I wanted... to receive!

It wasn't until I decided to stop hassling Dee about what she wasn't doing right and decided to give her the help she needed, with no expectations. That's when my prayer was answered. It was a lot of work during that time when I was trying to keep up with both my calendar and my wife's; but I will tell you it was truly worth it. We are more productive now as a husband and wife team than we have ever been. Our marriage just keeps getting better and better. Why? Because, I give what I want... to receive!

I will end this chapter by going back to the initial story. I went on to ask my relative, if the people at the church, where the pastor encouraged the people to give in two different envelopes, were being blessed. She thought about it for a minute and said, "Yes, both the pastor and the people seemed to be very blessed."

While it can be debated over whether it's biblical or not to support giving offerings in two different envelopes with a separate offering for the pastor, there is no debate over the biblical principle we are discussing here. You see, I give what I want... to receive. The people received a blessing because they gave cheerfully and with an understanding of this universal principle. I give what I want... to receive!

Earlier I gave you some words to live by and one of the passages says, "Do not be deceived: God cannot be mocked. A man reaps what he sows" (Galatians 6:7). While that, in and of itself, is a powerful passage; the one just above it is just as powerful. It reads, "Anyone who receives instruction in the word must share all good things with his instructor" (Galatians 6:6).

You see, this principle works no matter where you apply it. Whether it's in your relationship with your spouse, your boss at work, your parents, vegetables you plant in your garden or your money. I will always reap exactly what I sow; or in other words, I give what I want... to receive!

Now let's switch gears and take a look at a challenge facing just about every relationship that I know of in some way or another. After looking at the challenge, we will then explore the solutions.

Ω

What Every Woman Needs to Hear,
What Every Man Needs to Know

Questions for Group Discussion

1. What are one or two areas of disagreement in our relationship that seem to keep coming up over and over again?

2. What are one or two practical ways for me to "give" to my covenant partner what I want to "receive"?

Couple Exercise:

Use the "The Seven Steps to Resolving Disagreements" to resolve each area.

-2-

Sharing God's Forgiveness

"God is not always doing the same thing all the time"

The word challenge, by definition, is a call or summons to engage in any contest, as of skill or strength. A challenge, by its very nature, serves as a call to battle. A call to fight! So many times that's just what women and men do in their relationships... they fight!

It was about 10 p.m. when our flight landed in Freeport, Grand Bahamas. My wife, Dee, and I were scheduled to teach for three days in a marriage conference. That's the foundation of our ministry; we minister to marriages and the Lord has truly gifted us in this area.

When our Bahamian host greeted us at the airport he quickly announced to us the theme of the conference had changed. He told us the new theme of the conference would be..."Happy Husband and Wife, Happy Life." I can see you saying to yourself, so what? What's the big deal about a theme?

Well the big deal is, the year before Dee and I had ministered in that same conference for two days and we taught from a slightly different theme which was, "Happy wife...Happy life!" Apparently we had struck a chord and the pastor was intent on bringing balance to that statement.

As we soon learned, the underlying challenge the pastor had was much larger than one statement from a visiting minister. The challenge was deep. The challenge was wide. And yes, the challenge was long. The challenge was primarily... tradition!

Freeport Grand Bahamas is a beautiful tropical vacation paradise. It has a wonderful coastline populated with palm trees and some of the best beaches on the planet. It is also one of the top vacation spots in the world and has some of the friendliest people that you would ever want to meet. So what's the rub? That's all the stuff we see on the outside; but what about what's really going on in the heart of the city.

Whenever my wife and I visit a new spot, we will try to see as much of the area as we can. We'll do a lot of the tourist type stuff. However, we always like to meet some of the locals and go inside the inner city to see both how they really live and how they "do life" together.

On our first trip to Freeport, we were very fortunate to meet a guy who worked as the onsite photographer at the hotel where we stayed. When we met each other for the first time, something special happened. Rarely do I meet someone for the first time and know we will have a long lasting relationship; however, this was that type of guy. Not only was he a photographer, but he was also a pastor at a local church and asked if we would come and speak at his church. We agreed to pray about it, because after all, we were on vacation.

After prayer and consideration, Dee and I knew we were supposed to speak at his church. We also knew what we were to speak about. Back at home, we had just concluded teaching one of the most powerful teaching series we had ever taught which was entitled…What Every Woman Needs to Hear and What Every Man Needs to Know.

The teaching series had been extremely successful and had truly blessed and prospered many marriages. This is a message so profound that it will literally loosen the chains and set people free. However, they must first want to be free.

I knew the Lord was telling me we must teach this message, at this time, to these wonderful people in Freeport. As the time drew near we were sensing something very powerful was about to happen. And it did!

We taught and preached for two days and the atmosphere was explosive. It appeared almost everyone at the conference, including the pastor and his wife, were coming up asking for a prayer of deliverance. They were trapped in marriages steeped in religious, cultural and male-dominated tradition; tradition taught by man and not by God.

The revelation that God had given us to share with the people is that God had not given dominion to "males" alone, but had given dominion to both males and females. In addition, we are instructed to dominate and rule everything on the earth, with the exception of one thing, and that is... each other.

> So God created man in his own image,
> in the image of God created he him;
> male and female created he them.
> And God blessed them, and God said
> unto them, Be fruitful, and multiply,
> and replenish the earth, and subdue it:
> and have dominion over the fish of the
> sea, and over the fowl of the air, and
> over every living thing that moveth
> upon the earth.
>   - Genesis 1:27-28

When we see the word man in the statement, "...God created man in his own image," that is a Hebrew word which means male and female. In other words, the statement is really saying, "So God created males and females in his own image."

Now fundamentally we can all see the truth in that statement. In fact, most men don't have a problem with that statement. It's only when we continue down that passage, where it speaks of dominion, that some men have a problem.

In some cases, we have seen where men want to be the dominant player in the relationship. We have also seen in many cases where women feel as though their husbands are dominating them in their relationship. This is a bad model and it must be stopped! God told us [men] to love our wives and he told our wives [women] to respect their husbands. Now that's the model!

> However, each one of you also must
> love his wife as he loves himself, and
> the wife must respect her husband.
>   - Ephesians 5:33

In his book entitled "Love and Respect," Dr. Emerson Eggerichs wrestled with a sometimes-overlooked command from God. He came up with an insight that created three thoughts. The first thought he wrestled with was:

> "A husband is to obey the command to love even if his wife does not obey this command to respect, and a wife is to obey the command to respect even if the husband does not obey the command to love."

After meditating on that thought, Dr. Eggerirch went on to refine his thought process and wrote:

> A husband is even called to love a disrespectful wife, and a wife is called to respect an unloving husband. There is no justification for a husband to say, "I will love my wife *after* she respects me" nor for a wife to say, "I will respect my husband *after* he loves me."

Based on my many years as a relationship counselor, I could quickly see how both of these thoughts were true. I also understood both the biblical and relational significance of the two thoughts and had even taught and shared both sentiments on a number of occasions. However, it wasn't until Dr. Eggerichs gave his third thought that I got the answer to what so many of our couples had been struggling with. The third thought was this: "Without love, she reacts without respect. Without respect, he reacts without love."

Let's look at Ephesians 5:33 again:

> However, each one of you also *must* love his wife as he loves himself, and the wife *must* respect her husband
> - Ephesians 5:33(emphasis added)

I intentionally emphasized the word "must" here because I believe therein we find our answer. Why would the Lord command a man to love his wife and a wife to respect her husband? We don't see a request here, but rather a command. Could it be that the mystery of marriage that Paul talked about is found in those very words? Could it be that God knows how he made us and that's why he made this a commandment and not a request? Could it be the only way that we are going to find the peace in our home and the contentment we seek in a mate is to abide by this one very simple commandment? I believe the answer is a resounding YES!

My wife and I have literally taught, counseled and mentored thousands of couples, both individually and in larger settings, and there is one very consistent thing we see. The woman has a primary need for love while the man has a primary need for respect. We've seen this play out time after time after time. It's a tendency so prevalent that to ignore it could fall under the category of what we could only refer to as relational suicide.

I can remember one couple we mentored who had been married about three years. They were having serious communication issues in their marriage. The wife had grown up in a single parent home with her mother. After seeing her mom and dad go through a divorce, the dad just left and she didn't see much of him from that point.

We went on to find out that not only did her dad leave, but she also witnessed that same tendency of men leaving in many other relationships in her family as she was growing up.

On the other hand, her husband had grown up in a family where his parents had been together for almost forty years. While he didn't agree with everything his parents did and how they always responded to one another; he told us he did see a lot of respect from his mother towards his father.

Whenever this couple would get into a heated argument, he would threaten to leave and would even make the statement, "If you don't want me here, then I will leave." She would find herself hardening every time he would make such a statement and the argument would blow up to the point where either she would totally shut down or he would leave in order to go and blow off some steam.

They couldn't see it at the time, but their issue was all about love and respect. He couldn't see he needed to show his love for her by letting her know that he was committed to their relationship for the long haul and leaving was not an option. In fact, he had never heard her story about how much pain she felt over the men in her family, seemingly always leaving their women. She, on the other hand, couldn't see how she was pushing him out the door by her constant disrespectful, nagging and argumentative ways. She didn't know respect was what he most desired from her and when he didn't get respect his first thought was to hit the door.

Once they could see from each other's perspective, they began to love and respect one another in new ways. Their communication improved dramatically almost overnight and they have prospered greatly as a couple and as a family. She wrote these words to me in a note, that I use with her permission:

> I have really grown a lot spiritually through your teachings. I have really been seeking God to make sure that I am hearing his voice. I thought that when you hear from God, I was supposed to hear this deep voice that I was going to have this conversation with. But most of the time, I hear from him through scripture or through my notes, or just one of your messages. I guess what I am asking is, how could this possibly happen? Also, I want to thank you and Mrs. Dee for the counseling session. It really has changed my life. I am now more confident in myself and my relationship with my husband. I had never taken the time to figure out why certain things were bothering me, but now I know and understand. I am praying even more for God to continue to help me so that I may help others, especially my family.

This wife can "see" now. She can see how taking the time to learn how to communicate by respecting her husband has made all the difference. She also knows that her family has a history of marriages that end in separations or divorces and she is determined to change that pattern, both for herself and for others in her family.

As for our friends in the Bahamas, this is the truth of... What Every Woman Needs to Hear and What Every Man Needs to Know. We have not been put here on God's green earth to try and dominate one another. Rather we should look to honor one another by searching for ways to understand and encourage one another. Hebrews 10:24 says, "Let us consider how we may spur one another on toward love and good deeds." This is the truth that would eventually set all of our friends in covenant relationships free to be all that God had purposed them to be. However, the question remains, "Would they be ready?"

That's why when we were invited to speak the second year in Freeport the pastor quickly informed me that some of the women had been going "crazy," as he phrased it, with this newfound revelation that God had also given them dominion. He didn't know what else to do, so he changed the theme of the conference from "Happy Wife...Happy Life" to "Happy Husband and Wife, Happy Life."

Initially I reasoned that somehow, in his mind, he was wrestling with this new knowledge of women as equals and not subordinates. This knowledge went contrary to his tradition and the male-dominant culture he had grown up in. Somehow, in his mind, I thought, he knew the truth of what God's Word said, but he wanted to keep some of the old tradition; especially the part that made him feel superior to his wife. I eventually came to the realization however that in a very fundamental way, he was right.

When we taught in the prior year, I was early into the insight that God was birthing in me and maybe, just maybe I had given it to them prematurely. And if not prematurely, than certainly we may have not given it the proper balance that it deserved.

On the other hand, maybe they had gotten exactly what they needed at that time in order to trigger the necessary steps that would lead to their deliverance. Regardless, the pastor was right.

For us to know God gave dominion to both males and females is not incorrect, but it is incomplete. We must balance this knowledge with the understanding that a man is to love his wife and a wife is to respect her husband. Again as Dr. Eggerichs points out, "Without love, she reacts without respect. Without respect, he reacts without love."

Fortunately the cat had already been let out the bag the prior year and there was no turning back. Today is a new day! Today is a glorious day that the Lord has made and we will ALL rejoice and be glad in it. However, now is the time to deal with that very challenging issue we touched on earlier which is, namely, tradition.

Traditions are customs and practices from the past which are passed on as accepted standards of behavior for the present. Jesus criticized the Pharisees for slavishly following their traditions and making them more authoritative than the Scripture. Just like our

21

Bahamian friends were stuck in some male-dominant traditions that needed to be dealt with, we too so often find ourselves dealing with traditions of the past that are just not... of God.

In the Christian story, it is recorded:

> ...some Pharisees and teachers of the law came to Jesus from Jerusalem and asked, "Why do your disciples break the tradition of the elders? They don't wash their hands before they eat!" Jesus replied, "And why do you break the command of God for the sake of your traditions? For God said, 'Honor your father and mother' and 'Anyone who curses his father or mother must be put to death.' But you say that if a man says to his father or mother, 'Whatever help you might otherwise have received from me is a gift devoted to God,' he is not to 'honor his father' with it. **Thus you nullify the word of God for the sake of your tradition."**
> – Matthew 15:1-6

Jesus makes it very clear tradition is so powerful that it will literally make the Word of God null, void and ineffective in our lives. One point I would like to make note of here, with a promise to emphasize it more later on, is that love and respect are just due. They don't have to be earned. In other words, I owe Dee my love whether she has earned it or not. Likewise, I am due respect from Dee whether I have earned it or not. Love and respect are due just because God commanded it. Anything else is a tradition of man and not of God.

Remember, Jesus has already warned us that the one thing more powerful than the Word of God is the traditions of men we make more important than the Word. Herein we find one of the very first challenges we must overcome, and we will seek to do so in the next chapter.

Ω

What Every Woman Needs to Hear,
What Every Man Needs to Know

Questions for Group Discussion

1. What is love from a female perspective?

2. What is respect from a male perspective?

3. What are one or two things we do out of tradition that seem to create challenges in our relationship?

4. How do we currently share leadership in our relationship?

-3 -

Tradition

*"It is what it is, but it doesn't
have to always be that way."*

In this chapter you will meet three couples doing extremely well in their relationships. However, it hasn't always been so. You see they were all faced with some concerns that they hadn't dealt with. The concerns were all different, yet they all fell under the same category - tradition.

Tradition, in our context, has to deal with how we take from what we've learned and experienced in our past and bring it into our current relationship. In other words, how we handle our finances or our how we discipline our kids will have a lot to do with how we were taught to handle those situations. The couples you are about to meet had issues with the following:

- How to discipline kids in a blended family [kids from prior marriages and/or relationships]
- How to handle personality issues
- How to handle issues on religion

While issues of tradition can fall into a number of different areas, the answers are always the same; communicate, communicate, communicate and then come to agreement.

Our first couple, Mark and Susan, had been living together for almost a year when they came to us. They were engaged to be married and were looking for premarital counseling. Mark had been in a previous marriage which lasted almost fifteen years. He had one son who was fifteen years old. Susan had been married twice before. She had three children from the previous marriages ages twelve, eight and three.

Mark grew up in a home with a single mother and his dad would visit occasionally; however his dad was never a big part of his life. Mark said that the rules in his house growing up were fairly relaxed and he could basically do whatever he pleased. He had raised his fifteen year old son in a similar manner and thought that he was turning out just fine until his mother and Mark got divorced. That's when he saw another side of his fifteen year old son that was very disrespectful, from Mark's perspective.

Susan grew up in a home with both a mother and a father; however, her mom had been previously married and the father Susan grew up with was not her biological dad. In any event, her stepfather was her father in her mind. He was the one who provided for and gave them the discipline they needed. She remembered him as a strong disciplinarian and the rules were fairly rigid in their home. She would have to say where she was going, who she would be with, how long she would be gone and what time her parents could expect her to be home. She had a strict curfew and any deviation would be met with a punishment. The rules, as she remembered them, were rigid, but fair.

Dee and I asked them to tell us the biggest challenge they were facing at the time and without thinking twice, they both agreed it was the children. Mark had tried to discipline Susan's oldest son once and he was met with resistance from not only the son, but also from Susan. After the son had received some counseling from Mark, he then went to Susan to plead his case and she sided with her son. Susan then went to Mark and let him know, although in a loving way, she didn't appreciate the way he had dealt with the situation. Mark in turn became very irritated with Susan for allowing her twelve year old son to come between them.

Dee and I asked them if this was an isolated situation or if they had seen this pattern play out over and over again in their relationship. After thinking about it for a moment, they agreed it was a pattern. They had seen it not only with Susan's children, but also with Mark's son as well. They had noticed the friction not only in their relationship, but also a similar type of friction with Mark's ex-wife and Susan's ex-husband's when it came to the children.

Dee and I went on to share with them that we had seen this pattern over and over and over again when it came to blended families. Blended families are defined as families that were traditionally known as stepfamilies.

Blended families or stepfamilies seem to experience many struggles and sometimes have problems finding solutions to those problems. In fact, statistics say that about 60% of blended families will not survive the issues of ex-partners, step-children, in-laws and the different parenting styles. However, the good news we have found is that there are a few things that separate the successful blended families from the ones that give up, cave in and quit.

The keys are communication and coming to agreement. We asked both Mark and Susan to first look in the mirror. In other words, to look at the family or environment from which they originated. This is known as their family-of-origin. Once they did that, we then advised they ask themselves two simple questions over and over again.

1. What do I like about my family-of-origin that I want to bring into my current family?

2. What do I disliked about my family-of-origin that I don't want to bring into my current family?

As Mark and Susan continued to communicate and ask themselves those two simple questions over and over again, they found that most of their issues were derived from what they had experienced in past relationships or what they had been taught in their family-of-origin. Once they communicated what they liked and disliked and then came to agreement on how they wanted their new family to operate, their issues started to become much more manageable.

The issues have not all gone away; however, Mark and Susan now have a strategy of how to handle them. Their strategy is working not only for them, but for so many of the couples we mentor. Remember to communicate, communicate, communicate and then come to agreement.

27

Our second couple Fred and Amy were a perfect definition of the old saying, "opposites attract." Fred was very laid back, conservative and didn't have an outgoing personality. He was more of an introvert and he liked being to himself.

Fred had grown up in a family with two older brothers and no sisters. His mom had re-married when he was young and they grew up as a happy and very normal family, as Fred remembered it. They celebrated most of the major holidays, but he could remember when times were tight financially he and his brothers would often share gifts or maybe just get something simple for birthdays and Christmas.

Amy on the other hand, was a single child in a fairly well-to-do family. She was very outgoing and remembered birthdays and Christmas as some of her most fond memories. She had grown up with both her biological parents and she was the apple of her daddy's eye. She got just about anything she wanted as a child and her birthday was then, and still is now, a big deal to her parents.

When they came to see Dee and me, they were like a breath of fresh air. Most of the couples we see seem to wait until things are so bad they need major surgery to make things better. If only they had come earlier when maybe an aspirin would have done the trick. This couple actually only needed an aspirin.

When Fred and Amy came to their first session, they let us know they were having problems in their communications and it seemed as though their problems never really got resolved. When they attempted to resolve an issue it would inevitably lead to a conflict and they would find themselves not speaking to each other for a while. Therefore, it seemed avoiding the issue was how they handled it until they found that wasn't working either. As an unknown theologian once said, "Until you handle it with grace, it's going to stay in your face."

After spending just a little time with Fred and Amy, we asked them to work on what we like to call, "a third alternative." There is my way, there is your way or maybe if we work together and diligent search we can find "a third alternative."

We advised Fred and Amy to ask two questions of themselves.

1. What are three things your partner is currently doing that you like?

28

2. What are three things you would like to see your partner do more or less often?

The first question is designed to look at the positives. There is always, and I mean always, something positive we can talk about if we look hard enough. When relationships tend to get in trouble; however, it seems the focus is always on the negative aspects of the relationship. We also use this exercise and this time to let couples know we want to celebrate the positives and work on the opportunities [negatives].

When Fred and Amy began to work on this exercise, they found the very things that drew them to one another have now become a source of frustration. For instance, one thing Fred liked about Amy before they got together was her positive, upbeat and out-going personality. He said it helped to draw him out of his shell and he just liked being around so much enthusiasm early in their relationship.

Likewise, Amy commented that it was Fred's laid back personality and his stability that she liked in him. While he wasn't as outgoing as she was, he was very sure of himself and dependable. She could always depend on him.

Somewhere along the way, they had forgotten what originally attracted them to one another and had started to try and change each other. Amy was always on Fred about being more assertive and trying to get him to go out with her more. Fred, on the other hand, was trying to get Amy to spend more time at home with just the two of them. He did not like her always having the need to go out and be with her friends and/or her family. However, in constantly trying to change one another, they found themselves at odds with each other and the conflict at times seemed unbearable.

Once they began to communicate by asking just those two questions, they began to start seeing from the other's perspective. Once they started to see from each other's perspective, they began to create that third alternative. That third alternative for them was for both of them to give a little bit without bending or breaking. Fred began to go out with Amy more, but they would also agree not to be the last ones to leave the party. Fred could only take so much.

29

Amy agreed to spend more quality time with Fred at home - just the two of them. Sometimes that meant not talking on the phone or taking calls when they were in quality time alone. Other times that meant saying no to some friends or family that wanted her time. Likewise, Amy could only take so much so Fred did not become too overbearing. They kept a nice balance and it made all the difference. Their communication improved and the conflict they were experiencing went down dramatically. Remember, there must be balance in all things and we will talk about that a great deal more in chapter 5.

Our third couple, Cindy and Jim, came to see us after about five years of a very troubled marriage. Cindy had grown up Catholic and Jim had grown up in a Muslim home. They had a little boy, John, who was almost three years old and they both seemed to love him very much.

They seemed to find themselves arguing over just about everything. If Jim wanted fish for dinner, it seemed as though Cindy would have a taste for chicken. If Cindy wanted to go to a movie, Jim would be head strong about watching a football game. If they had a conversation about their finances, it seemed to always end in an argument. They argued about who would pick little John up from the daycare and who would drop him off. They argued about who would cook, clean or even take out the trash. They seemed to argue about everything!

Jim had grown up in a traditional Muslim home where he saw his father go off to work and his mother would stay home and take care of the household and the needs of the children. Cindy on the other hand had grown up in a home where both of her parents worked professional jobs and they shared just about all of the household responsibilities. While they couldn't see it at the time, they were both stuck in some traditions they learned as they were growing up.

Jim had a very strict religious upbringing and he couldn't wait to go to college where he was free, as he phrased it, "not to go to religious" gatherings. On the other hand, while Cindy had gone to Catholic schools growing up, her parents rarely made going to Mass a part of their week. They would go maybe on holidays or special occasions such as weddings or baptisms.

Cindy and Jim met in college and while there, they seemed to be of one accord. However, it was after their marriage and moving back closer to Jim's parents that things seemed to get rough.

While Jim could get away with going to a religious gathering infrequently at college, he was almost expected to attend weekly gatherings at home. It was their family tradition. While Cindy didn't mind Jim attending as frequently as he wanted, she would have no part of being a good Muslim wife by attending and adhering to the traditions of Jim's faith. In fact, had she known it was a part of the deal going into the marriage she suggested she might have thought twice before saying, "yes."

Can you see how tradition plays a big part in this couples relationship? While we chose to give you an example of religious traditions here, it could have been just about anything. It could have been politics, race, culture, economics, food preferences, sex, how we raise the kids, which holidays we celebrate or don't celebrate, how we manage money, and the list goes on and on and on.

Tradition plays a large role in any relationship because each individual comes from a set of values. The things we value tend to guide our decision making process and ultimately make up who we are.

It wasn't until we had several discussions with Jim and Cindy and identified their inherent traditions and then compared those traditions to the things they both agreed they valued, that we could then help them come up with some new ones that fit their relationship. I won't say that it was easy, but since we were working with two individuals that deeply cared for one another and were willing to seek a WIN/WIN solution, it was achievable.

In the end, Jim and Cindy created their own family traditions which now guide guide their relationship. While their parents, on both sides, might not be as agreeable with all the decisions Jim and Cindy have reached, they are happy to see the wonderful progress the couple is making.

Not only were we faced with some issues of tradition between Jim and Cindy, but we were also faced with some questions of tradition from the perspective of Dee and me as counselors/mentors. You see, both Dee and I are Christians and in our tradition we have some very strong beliefs about who Christ is,

31

what He did and what He is still doing in both our lives and in the world. Our traditional beliefs bumped right up against what Jim believed as a Muslim.

When we were first asked to meet with this couple, Dee and I both spent time in prayer. We asked God for guidance on, first of all, if we should mentor this couple and if so, how would we mentor them. I was led to call a friend of mine named, Leo, who lived in Michigan. Leo is a strong Christian who has done an extensive amount of study on the Muslim faith. I told him our situation and he asked me a very profound question. He asked, "Are you going to meet with them to talk about religion, or are you meeting with them to talk about their relationship?"

After truly pondering that question for a while, I could honestly say, we were meeting with them to help them with their relationship. I can truly say that it turned out to be one of the most pleasant and enlightening experiences that we have had and I can also tell you without a shadow of a doubt... these principles work!

We would focus on God and not on religion. We would also only look at the first five books of the bible as our reference. It was something that we ALL could agree on and I believe with everything in me that God got the glory. We had some of the richest conversations that you could ever imagine and I know that the Holy Spirit participated in them all.

While we didn't meet with the couple initially with the intent of talking about religion, the couple was helped by seeing Christ being lived out in our lives. I believe God was pleased and Dee and I grew up just a little bit more as we allowed God to deal with tradition in a very wonderful way. God tells us very clearly that His thoughts are higher than our thoughts and that His ways are higher than our ways. What a mighty God we serve.

The primary challenge with tradition is that it goes so deep. In order to dig it up sometimes we, not only need a shovel, but also some heavy duty, earth moving equipment. The best way I have found to deal with tradition is with a heavy dose of the Word of God. With that in mind, let's start at the beginning.

In the book of Genesis, in the very first chapter, we read the words "And God said..." God said many things and the one thing that we see consistently throughout the entire bible is that whatever

God says, He eventually sees. Or in other words, whatever God says, eventually happens.

God said, "let there be light" and there was light. God said, "let there be animals" and there were animals. God said, "let seeds bear fruit after their own kind" and that's why we see apple seeds producing apples and orange seeds producing oranges. The seeds are producing after their own kind….just like God said.

And then God said, "Let us make man in our image, in our likeness, and let them rule [have dominion] over the fish of the sea and the birds of the air, over the livestock, over all the earth, and over all the creatures that move along the ground." So God created man in his own image, in the image of God he created him: **male and female he created them**. God blessed **them** and said to **them**, "Be fruitful and increase in number; fill the earth and subdue it. Rule [have dominion] over the fish of the sea and the birds of the air and over every living creature that moves on the ground."

When we see the word man in the above scripture, it is important to reiterate that it comes from a Hebrew word which means human being or human kind. It does not mean a male figure but denotes both male and female. In other words, when God gave the dominion mandate, it was not just to men. He gave dominion to both men and women; males and females. He gave us dominion over everything on the earth with the exception of just one thing… each other.

When we are stuck in tradition, in actuality we are stuck in our tendencies. A tendency by definition is a natural or prevailing disposition to move, proceed or act in some direction or toward some point, end or result. In other words, we are predisposed to act in a certain way. Our tendencies can be either good or bad; however, they are very powerful.

You see, when Jim had gone off to college, he had broken away from his tendency to attend religious services on a weekly basis. However, when he married and moved back home, he found he was predisposed to act in a certain way. Almost without trying or even knowing that he was doing it, he found himself moving in a certain direction. It again became a habit.

His wife Cindy, on the other hand, had a predisposition or a tendency to move in a direction totally opposite of Jim's and it led to conflict in their relationship. Again, I will restate that our tendencies can be either good or bad; however, they are very powerful.

It wasn't until Cindy stopped trying to impose her predisposition on Jim and Jim stopped trying to impose his tendency on her that they began to create new and more meaningful traditions. By agreeing first of all that neither of them would try to dominate the other they could then take the next step of having dominion together. With God's guidance, they became co-creators and began to create their own map in life.

While they had to shake off many of the traditions they had learned in the past, they are now operating in some new traditions which work for them as covenant partners. They are enjoying a newness of life that is free from all of the arguing and the bickering that used to prevail at their home.

While Jim and Cindy still have many questions to ponder about religion, traditions and purpose; at least they have a home with enough peace in it to enter into that next level of dialogue. Purpose will also be our next conversation. Why are we here?

What is the purpose of a woman? What is the purpose of a man? Only when tradition lines up with God's original purpose for a woman or for a man, can that tradition be considered as "of God." If our tradition is not in line with God's original purpose, it is "of man," or in other words, it is a tradition of man.

In Proverbs 19:21, the Bible tells us this. "Many are the plans in a man's heart, but it is the Lords purpose that prevails." In the next chapter, I want us to focus on that word, purpose. Let's spend some time now truly understanding what our purpose is and also what God's plan is for our lives.

Ω

What Every Woman Needs to Hear,
What Every Man Needs to Know

Questions for Couple or Group Discussion

1. What do I like about my family-of-origin that I want in my current family?

2. What do I dislike about my family-of-origin that I don't want in my current family?

3. What are three things my partner is doing that I like?

4. What are three things I would like to see my partner do more or less often?

-4-

Purpose

"Purpose is the original intent of the creator in the creation of something. It is what is in the creator's mind that causes him to fashion his product in a certain manner. In short, purpose motivates the action of creation. This results in precision production."
- Dr. Myles Monroe

What is the purpose of a woman? What is the purpose of a man? Only when tradition lines up with God's original purpose for a woman or for a man, can the tradition be considered as "of God." If our tradition is not in line with God's original purpose, it is "of man," or in other words, it is a tradition of man. *Many are the plans in a man's heart, but it is the Lord's purpose that will prevail.*

Men have had problems with women; and women have had problems with men even back in the days of the Bible. I believe there is an underlying reason for that and if you'll bear with me just for a little longer, I believe that you're going to understand where the issue derives from and why it's of the utmost importance that we solve it.

The Bible records the story of an encounter Jesus had with a Samaritan woman. If you can see the scene in your mind, a current day episode would look something like this. Jesus was sitting alone in middle of a mall. His followers had gone to the restaurant and had agreed to bring Jesus back some takeout. As Jesus was hanging out in the middle of the mall, a woman, of a different race, comes by and Jesus had the nerve to ask her if she would go and get him something to drink.

Now what is really so disturbing about this whole scene is that Jesus' family and her family had been in a family feud for several hundred years, I mean for generations. Jesus should know better than to ask her for anything. Now, not only had their families been feuding for generations; but there was at least one more issue that we need to pay attention to. Back in that time, women just didn't talk to men like that and especially not in public.

After the Samaritan woman had thoroughly enlightened Jesus of the seriousness of issues at hand, Jesus gave her a very interesting reply. He said, and I quote, "If you knew the gift of God and who it is that asks you for a drink, you would have asked him and he would have given you living water" (John 4:10).

When we are studying history and especially biblical history, it is important to understand at least two things to get a truer understanding of what was happening back in that day. Number one, we need to understand something about the culture of the people we are studying and secondly, we need to understand some of the traditions of the time.

In the context of this story, there are at least three traditions "of men" Jesus was challenged with. The first was women and men, in that day, just didn't get along very well. A Jewish man would not be caught speaking to woman in public. Secondly, the Samaritan people and the Jewish people did not associate with one another. The Jewish people considered the Samaritans to be a biracial or mixed breed of people and they did not have anything to do with them. Thirdly, there was the issue of class. This woman was truly not a woman of class; she had been married several times and the man she was now "shacking" with was not her husband.

Depending on who you are and how you were raised, some of these issues might be hard for you to believe; however, please remember it wasn't very many years ago (in the 1940's to be exact), that women in the United States got the right to vote. That's right, in the nation that is famous for its freedom and democracy it was only a short time ago women were given the right to vote. And if we were to speak of the racial issues that existed and still exist in America, that would take up several more chapters.

I said all that to say this; the traditions "of men" that Jesus had to overcome in his day have not all gone away. We too must be willing to deal with traditions of men in ALL their ugly forms and when we find they don't line up with God's original purpose for women and men, we too must confront them.

Bestselling author and pastor, Dr. Miles Monroe, made the statement, "If you don't know the purpose of a thing, abuse is inevitable." He goes on to suggest, purpose is the original intent of the Creator in the creation of something. What that says to me is when God created us he had to have an original intent.

When God created a man, he had an original intent. When God created a female, he had an original intent. God is a very purposeful God. He has a purpose for everything he ever created. Every living animal has a purpose. The sun has a purpose. The moon has a purpose. The rain has a purpose. The flowers and all the trees have a purpose. Even a tiny little seed has a purpose. God is a God of purpose and when he created us male and female, he had an original purpose in mind.

Only when we know the purpose of a woman, as men, will we stop abusing or being unloving towards her. Only when we know the purpose of a man, as women, will we stop abusing or being disrespectful towards him. Where the original purpose of something is not known, abuse is not far behind.

The purpose of something will determine both its nature and its design. The nature of something determines its functions and its needs. In order to truly understand the purpose of anything, it is important to go back to the manufacturer to understand what He intended when he created the thing.

When God created a woman, he made her relational to the core. When God created a man, he made him to be a leader and a provider. When we are functioning in our God-given roles we are operating at God's best for us. When we are not functioning in our purpose, it will have both temporary and sometimes even permanent effects.

I am reminded of a couple that we ministered to many years ago. The wife was very active in church and in fact she had just joined the staff of a local church that we were affiliated with. Her husband, at that time, did not belong to any church and he was seemingly very content with that status.

We would occasional see the husband, whom we will call Justin, at social functions, but that was about the extent of the contact that we had with him. He was always very pleasant when we would get together, but he was also always very guarded. He would never allow you to get too close to.

On one occasion his wife, who we will refer to as Susan, asked if I would reach out to him personally to see if he could be reached. At the time Justin was working as a manager in a local strip club and church folk were the last thing on his mind. I agreed to reach out and invite him to lunch.

Justin and I went to eat catfish at a local restaurant and we hit it off from day one. We continued to meet almost every week for about six months before we ever talked about church at all. We would just eat catfish and talk about life. As we got to know each other better and began to trust one another more, we began to speak about things of more value, such as Christ and the impact that Christ had made on my life.

I shared with Justin that for many years I had not been the spiritual leader in my home, but only the financial provider. I shared with him that not only had I been unfaithful to my wife, but I had also been an alcoholic. I shared with Justin that it was only after I received the message that Jesus not only saves us, but also has the power to change our lives in a very wonderful way, that I truly began to live. Once I received that message, my life has never been the same.

I went on to share with Justin that the message of Christ saving us and changing us was still only part of the good news. Once Christ saves us and changes us, we then become new creatures and all the old stuff we used to do can NEVER be counted against us. I explained to Justin that once we are in Christ, there is no condemnation. When Justin asked for some more specifics about condemnation, I shared the following thought I, like the Apostle Paul, now live by:

> Therefore, if anyone is in Christ, he is a new creation; the old has gone, the new has come!
> - 2 Corinthians 5:17

Or in other words, Apostle Paul is saying,

If you're blaming this guy, for what that old guy did, you're blaming the wrong guy!

The Random House College Dictionary defines the word condemnation as follows:

1. To pronounce adverse judgment on
2. To give grounds or reasons for convicting or for blame
3. To pronounce guilty or sentence to punishment
4. To judge or pronounce to be unfit for use or service
5. To declare incurable

When Jesus died for us, I explained to Justin, he cured us from all our sins; past, present and future. We are not unfit for use in his Kingdom or his service. No one, including ourselves, our spouses or anyone else, can pronounce use guilty or sentence us to any type of punishment. We are not to allow others to convict us or even blame us for anything we have done in our past. "If you're blaming this guy for what that guy did, you're blaming the wrong guy." In Romans 8:1-2, we read:

> Therefore, there is now no condemnation for those who are in Christ Jesus, because through Christ Jesus the law of the Spirit of life set me free from the law of sin and death.
> Romans 8:5-6, continues:

> Those who live according to the sinful nature have their minds set on what that nature desires; but those who live in accordance with the Spirit have their minds set on what the Spirit desires. The mind of sinful man is death, but the mind controlled by the Spirit is life and peace

I am happy to report that Justin received the message about Jesus Christ and he is allowing Jesus to change his life completely. Justin no longer works at the strip club, but is a minister of the Gospel of Jesus Christ. He has truly been transformed by the renewing of his mind. Unfortunately that's not the end of the story. Justin called me recently to say that he and his wife Susan are filing for a divorce. After a brief update from Justin, he said the following words:

> She has carried the spiritual weight in our family for so long, she doesn't know how to give it over

What Susan and Justin are experiencing, we see a lot. When Justin came into his proper role as the spiritual leader of his house, it presented a tremendous change in the family dynamics. The change was so quick and so drastic that Susan didn't know how to handle it.

You see Susan had always needed to carry the spiritual weight in their home, because if she didn't, no one would. However, once Justin renewed his mind to his proper purpose, it was time for them to sit down and redefine their relationship. While we will talk a great deal about this principle of redefining relationships in a subsequent chapter, it is important to note here that ALL relationships go through changes. Change happens and that's normal. The issues come when we don't see the shifts or changes in our relationship landscape and make the necessary adjustments. The issues will come, but always remember that they don't have to overcome!

The enemy will use any and every opportunity to try and divide us; even Jesus. In essence, Susan was "Jealous about Jesus." That's right, Jealous about Jesus. You see, Jesus is now #1 in Justin's life where before Susan held that spiritual spot. Now they must come together and understand where they are now. They are operating in purpose and although it looks and feels strange; they are right where they are suppose to be.

The good news is the jury is still out on Susan and Justin. They have filed for divorce, but haven't divorced yet so there is still hope. I think it's time to schedule another catfish lunch with Justin; however, this time we're going to invite Susan and Dee.

Dee and I have seen this same scene play out over and over and over again. The wife prays earnestly to God for her husband to come into a closer walk with Him. God honors that prayer and the husband comes into his proper role or purpose. The enemy then sneaks in to try and divide the couple.

The couple begins to compare themselves against one another to see who is the most spiritual. They start to compete against one another not knowing that they are headed for destruction. We even see them start to try and dominate one another by using the scriptures as the basis for their battles. The Apostle Paul warns us:

> We do not dare to classify or compare ourselves with some who commend themselves. When they measure themselves by themselves, they are not wise.
> - 2 Corinthians 10:12

When God gave us [males and females] the commandment to rule and have dominion, it was His intent for us to do it together and not for us to be in competition with one another. We each have a role to play and our roles are vital. One is not any more important than the other and we need each other in order to function correctly and to have dominion. I believe dominion is the essence of the mystery the Bible talks about when we are told "the two shall become one." When we are one in spirit, we are powerful and dominion is inevitable; however, we must both function in our roles.

In the mind of God, he gave the man positional authority, while he gave the woman influence authority. While we will discuss these two concepts in much more depth in the next chapter, it is important to note that when they work together in perfect unity, there is a balance that is so powerful it is virtually unstoppable. And that's what we are going to focus on next... balance in ALL things!

Ω

What Every Woman Needs to Hear,
What Every Man Needs to Know

Questions for Couple or Group Discussion

1. What is the original purpose of a woman?

2. What is the original purpose of a man?

3. How has society and circumstances tried to redefine God's original purpose?

Balance In ALL Things

"As long as the earth endures,
seedtime and harvest,
cold and heat,
summer and winter,
day and night
will never cease"
-Genesis 8:22

God is a God of order. We can see God's order everywhere we look. When we look at the stars and the moon, we see perfect order. When we see the sun in relationship to the moon, again we see order. When we evaluate the relationship between night and day or the rain and the sunshine or seedtime and harvest or even between summer and winter; there is always order. The nighttime never says to the daytime, "Let me go first." Why... because God has created perfect order between them. Well if God went to such great length to create order in the universe wouldn't it just seem logical He would also give us a way to create order in our relationships?

All throughout the scriptures we see God's order. Another way to say that is we see God's way of doing things. So naturally we should believe God has an order to our relationships. I believe God did this so that we might keep balance and harmony in our relationships. God also created order in such a way as to not make it complicated.

In a marriage relationship, God gave the man positional authority; and God gave the woman influential authority. Before we explain exactly what positional and influential authority should look like, let's first understand what authority is.

By definition, authority means the power or right to do something, particularly to give orders and see that they are followed. However, the word authority as used in the Bible usually means a person's right to do certain things because of the position or office held by that person. There are basically two forms of authority; intrinsic or derived.

Intrinsic authority is authority that belongs to one's essential nature or in other words you were born with it. Derived authority, on the other hand, is authority that has been given to you from some other [man-made] source. For the majority of our discussion regarding authority, we will be discussing intrinsic authority, which is authority you were born with, or authority that has been given to us by God.

To the man, God gave positional authority; and to the woman, God gave influential authority. Since authority has been given to us by God and not derived from some other man-made source; that authority is a part of our nature. It's how God designed us and therefore it's just who we are.

It's extremely important I make a point of clarification here. This conversation we are in right now is mainly about a marriage and how God has created order in a marriage relationship. I am not saying a woman will never have a role of positional authority; nor am I saying a man will never find himself in a role that has influential authority. That is not the intent of this discussion. I point this out as not to offend anyone. If an offense occurs, it has been my experience that little, if anything, else will be heard. This is one of the most important topics in this entire book and it is my prayer you will continue reading and hear the conclusion of the matter.

I believe if we, especially as married couples, understand this one principle, we will change in a very powerful way. God knew what he was doing when he created us and if we tap into this mystery our marriages and other covenant relationships will grow in ways we never even imagined. So whatever you do, don't turn off. Listen and see what the end is going to look like. I think you'll be pleasantly surprised.

The Wife has Influential Authority

I can remember early one morning when we were right in the middle of completing our first book, *Empowering Right Relationships: First to God and Then to One Another*, that my wife came to me and said these very words. "You don't care about the children." I immediate retorted, "What do you mean, I don't care about the children. I love the children." She went on to tell me that if I cared about the children, as much as I did the book I was writing, than we would buy the building right next door to our church for our children's ministry.

Within just one week, I had not only scheduled a meeting with a representative of the bank that owned the building, but we had also entered into preliminary discussions about the possibility of us purchasing the building.

A couple of really important things we need to know about that story. First of all our church was only about a year old at the time and we had just taken on a $1.2 million dollar debt to purchase the church building we were currently in. Secondly, our church had not grown to the point where we needed the building next door for our children's ministry, albeit, it would have been nice to secure.

I said all that to emphasize a point. Basically, it made no logical sense for me to schedule the meeting to discuss buying another building when we could barely pay for the current one. However, because of my wife's powerful influence over me, I wanted to **make it happen!**

Now to be totally fair to my wife, she didn't know all the details of the finances of the church. She was just passionate about getting all the resources available to help teach the children. You see, our mission at our church is, "To Empower Right Relationships, Share God's Love and Teach the Children." That's all that Dee was focused on - teaching those children. Thus, when she saw the building next door she saw it as an excellent opportunity to help with that piece of our mission.

My point here is not to say who was right or wrong in this particular situation. The message; however, I would like to convey is the powerful influence a woman has in a marriage. The word influence means having the capacity or power to produce effects on others by intangible or indirect means. It means to compel, sway, induce or persuade someone into action. This is exactly the influence a respectful wife has with her husband.

This message really shouldn't be a surprise to any of us because it has been this way since the beginning:

> When the woman [Eve] saw that the fruit of the tree was good for food and pleasing to the eye, and also desirable for gaining wisdom, she took some and ate it. *She also gave some to her husband [Adam],who was with her, and he ate it.*
>   -Genesis 3:6

Most of us have heard the story of Adam and Eve, the first two people that ever lived. God placed them in a beautiful garden and made available many things to satisfy their appetites. However, God said to Adam, not to eat from just one tree; which was called the tree of the knowledge of good and evil. Now keep in mind that every other tree was okay to eat from; however, just this one tree was off limit.

While many people have written about how the woman, Eve, was the one who was deceived into eating from the forbidden tree, please also note, with great care, that Adam was right there with her the whole time. Remember also that the command not to eat from the forbidden tree was not given directly to Eve, but to Adam.

Let's also pay keen attention to at least one other important fact. The serpent, of which God said was craftier than any of the wild animals he had made, chose Eve to have his conversation with. I believe the serpent knew if he could convince Eve to eat from the tree, she could influence Adam. The serpent knew that by her very nature, the woman had an influence on Adam. I heard it once said like this, "If the man is the head, than the woman is the neck. And it is always the neck that turns the head." In other words, she has influence authority.

This story has been repeated over and over throughout the Bible and throughout all of human history. Abraham, who many of us know as the father of faith, was influenced by his wife Sarah to have a son by their servant, whose name was Hagar. Hagar did give birth to a son and she named him Ishmael. You see, Sarah, like many of us, thought that God was just taking a little bit too long to deliver on the promise he had made to her husband Abraham; that they would have a son in their old age. Therefore, Sarah took matters into her own hands and influenced her husband to have a son another way.

Abraham did eventually have the son God promised with his wife Sarah and they named him Isaac. When Isaac was born, Sarah again influenced Abraham.

> ... Sarah saw that the son whom Hagar the Egyptian had borne to Abraham was mocking, and she said to Abraham, "Get rid of that slave woman and her son, for that slave woman's son will never share in the inheritance with my son Isaac.
> - Genesis 21:9-10

We are told in another passage that these instructions from Sarah distressed Abraham in a very great way. His wife Sarah was telling him to get rid of his son and the woman who gave birth to him. Could you imagine how Abraham must have felt? However we are then told Abraham heard these words from God.

> ...Listen to whatever Sarah tells you, because it is through Isaac that your offspring will be reckoned."
> - Genesis 21:12

It is my belief and it has also been my experience that these are some of the most powerful words in scripture. "Listen to whatever Sarah tells you..." Abraham listened to his wife first and then got validation from God.

One of the biggest issues we see in marriages today is men just don't listen. Our wives have been gifted by God to be our helpers and if only we would listen. Many times the excuse we hear is that if Adam had not listened to Eve we wouldn't be in this mess. While that's not necessarily incorrect, it is definitely incomplete.

If Adam had listened to Eve and then checked with God, we wouldn't be in this mess. Women were designed and purposed by God, to speak into the lives of men and speak in a very powerful way. It is then incumbent upon the man to check with God for validation. When God created the woman, he had a very specific purpose in mind. God said:

> It is not good for the man to be alone. I will make a helper suitable for him.
> -Genesis 2:18

The word helper here comes from the Hebrew word, *EZER*. If we were to take that word and have some fun with it, we could make the case that God gave the man a woman to make his life E-Z –ER [**easier**].

EZER means to help, assist or aid. In fact the word is mentioned (21) times in the Old Testament of the Bible and with the exception of only two times, it always referred to God. That's right, the helper was God. One passage says, "I look to the hills, from which comes my help. My help comes from the Lord."

In most of the other biblical passages we also see God as our helper. However in the book of Genesis, the two times the word *EZER* or *helper* was mentioned it did not refer to God, but rather it referred to a woman. In other words, God made for the man a helper that closely resembled Himself.

In fact that truly has to be the case. God said he would make a helper suitable for the man or in other words, he would make someone to help make his life **easier**. I have truly found this to be true as I've learned to listen to my wife and then check with God. They usually agree! When they don't agree, I will simply ask my wife about how much time she's spending with God. Since God is Spirit and there is only ONE God, then we should be hearing the same thing.

God designed a woman in such a way that she is relational to the core. That's why a man is commanded in the New Testament to love his wife. In fact the man is not only commanded to love his wife, but he is commanded to love his wife with an unconditional love.

The reason for this is simple. The man is commanded to love his wife unconditionally because God knew how he designed and purposed a woman. A woman is relational to the core and she responds or reacts best when she feels loved. Nowhere in the New Testament do we see a command for the women to love her husband. Why, you might ask? It is because a woman IS love. She was designed that way from the beginning. There is no need for God to command her to do what she already is by nature.

Let's go back to that word helper or *E-Z-ER*. God created a helper for the man to make his life easier. That word helper again as it was used in this context was mentioned twenty-one (21) times in the Old Testament of the Bible. In the book of Genesis it refers to a female as the helper, of a man. Every other time the word is mentioned it is in reference to God. For instance:

God is our refuge and strength, an ever-present help in trouble
-Psalms 46:1

We wait in hope for the Lord; he is our help and our shield.
-Psalms 33:20

I lift up my eyes to the hills- where does my help come from? My help comes from the Lord, the Maker of heaven and earth.
-Psalms121:1-2

Because the Sovereign Lord helps me, I will not be disgraced. Therefore have I set my face like flint, and I know I will not be put to shame.
-Isaiah 50:7

God is love and the closet reflection of God on this earth is a woman. Now that is both a profound and a very powerful statement. And yet it is so true.

When God said, He would make the man a helper that was suitable for him; in essence He was saying, I will make for the man someone who resembles Me. Just like God, a woman is relational to the core. Just like God, who is love, a woman is love by her very nature. Just like God, a woman is a nurturer. She gives birth to a child and then sees to it that the child is nurtured. She is all about relationships, just like God.

Just as a man is commanded to love his wife, because that's what she responds best to. Likewise, a woman is commanded to respect her husband, because that's what he responds best to. Just as a man is commanded to love his wife with an unconditional love, likewise, a wife is commanded to respect her husband unconditionally.

The reason, again stated very simply, is because God knew how he designed and purposed a man. A man has been designed to both treasure and respond to respect. A woman is not commanded to love her husband because that would just be redundant. Love is who she is. However, she is commanded to respect her husband because God knows that at the very core of a man's being, he longs for respect. Without it, he is devastated.

Recently I asked myself the question, "Is there something I can do to earn God's blessing or God's favor?" While we can spend from now until the end of eternity debating the answer; there is something about God's love, grace and favor that he just gives to us... unearned. In fact, the definition of grace is "unmerited" or "unearned" favor from God.

Unfortunately, in our culture, for the most part, we are taught that while we might be able to give love unconditionally; respect is something that must be earned. This is a real problem in many relationships. A wife has a desire to be loved by her husband, while at the same time she is waiting for her husband to earn her respect. By doing so, she is burdening him with the tasks of both giving her what she most desires (love), and at the same time asking him to work hard to earn what he desires most (respect). It's just too much for him. Remember the Lord told us that he would never give us more than we can bear. In the passage below, we are reminded that:

> No temptation has seized you except what is common to man. And God is faithful; he will not let you be tempted beyond what you can bear. But when you are tempted, he will also provide a way out [make a way to escape] so that you can stand up under it.
> -1 Corinthians 10:13

Having the responsibility for both love and respect in a relationship is more than a man can bear. This, quite frankly, is one of the reasons that over 50% of both Christian and non-Christian marriages are ending in divorce. When the pressure becomes more than he can bear, he is diligently searching for a way out. As opposed to just doing his part in the relationship and loving his wife with an unconditional love, he would rather find a way of escape, hoping that next time will be better.

Please note, with great care, that I said this is one of the reasons that marriages end in divorce. While we know that there are many factors that lead people to make a decision to end their relationships, we have found this is definitely one of those factors. Fortunately, there is an answer.

A woman is to use her very powerful influence authority only in a way that gives unconditional respect for her husband. In other words, whether her husband has earned her respect or not; she is to give it to him. By no means am I asking a woman to become a doormat for her husband to do with her whatever foolish thing he desires. That is certainly not of God. However, what I am saying is there is tremendous power that comes on the woman when she follows this very simple prescription to respect her husband unconditionally. When she does so, a mystery will unfold right before her very eyes. The two shall become one and what a powerful one they will be. Now let me say just a few words to the men.

The Husband has Positional Authority

I can remember very vividly the time when we were taking our daughter, Dierdre, to college for her freshman year at the University of Alabama. We loaded up both my truck and her car for the journey. My wife Dee rode with Dierdre in her car, so I was looking forward to the three hour drive alone. I had planned to listen to some CD's and tapes and just enjoy the very scenic drive. Boy was I in for a surprise!

About thirty minutes into the trip, I got a call from my accountability partner and he said that he had been praying and wanted to share some things with me. An accountability partner is just that, someone you have in your life to keep you accountable for doing the right thing. My accountability partner and I had been in relationship with one another for about six years at that time and we knew each other very well.

He went on to share with me that he had some concerns about my leadership style. He said that he recently had a conversation with some of the former leaders at our church who had shared with him several concerns they had with my leadership style. He also let me know the former leaders wanted to remain anonymous.

He went on to share with me some of their concerns and as he did so, I felt myself very quickly starting to shut down and I began to go into a really defensive mode. I later wrote in my journal the following comments.

> I remember how I felt when my accountability partner attempted to speak into my life. I felt as if...
>
> 1. He didn't truly understand
> 2. He had pre-judged me
> 3. He was being manipulative
> 4. He was not a part of my vision; nor could he even see it
> 5. He was attacking me
> 6. He compared his goals in life to my vision (which was much bigger)
> 7. He was being very critical towards me
>
> While I believed very deeply in my heart that he had no ill intent; I still found myself being very offended by his words. I later wondered if that's how I make people feel when I speak truth into their lives. Whether our words are helpful or not (and his words have turned out to be very helpful); do we risk offending people to the point of no return? I believe the reason that my accountability partner could "go there" with me is because of our history together. Whether I liked what he said or not, he had earned the right to speak into my life.

While my accountability partner said words to me that were very hurtful at the time; those words have proven to be a difference maker in my life. I have since changed some things in my leadership style that have paved the way to many of the successes we are now enjoying in our ministry. Even having said this, I can still remember the pain of his words.

I believe that wives have that same place in the lives of husbands. They are an accountability partner for us. They know some things innately or intuitively that will prove to be very helpful to men. The rub comes in sometimes because, men just don't want to hear those words and especially from her. Sometimes, we as men feel exactly what I was feeling when my friend and accountability partner was speaking into my life.

Men; have you ever felt like your wife just doesn't understand you? Have you ever felt like she had pre-judged a situation or that she was in some way being manipulative? Have you ever felt like she just couldn't see what you saw at the time and she was focusing on the small details versus the big picture? Or, maybe you've felt as if she was attacking you in some way by her critical tone of voice. Does any of this sound a little too familiar?

It's not until we, as men, learn to truly value the words of our wife that they will get to that magical and somewhat mystical place in the relationship we so desire. We must remember that just like my accountability partner had no ill intent, our wives don't either. They only want what's best for us even when we can't see it at the time. That is why God commanded the man to love his wife. And men, please remember love is not sex.

Love is being patient with your wife. There are so many times I just want my wife to hurry up and get to the point. However, she communicates differently and I must be patient with her. Sometimes by just making that extra effort to hear and understand from her point of view makes all the difference.

Love is being kind to your wife. Kind is a relative word, so we must learn what kindness means to her. For instance, being kind to a man might mean making sure that dinner is prepared and waiting for him when he gets home. But if, by chance, you decided to cook a meal one day and have it ready when your wife got home, she would probably appreciate it very much; however, that might not be what she considers to be kindness.

Kindness to her might be for you to just be more aware. She wants you to notice things around your environment a lot more. Notice the garbage when it needs to be taken out. Notice the toilet seat when it needs to be let down. Notice the garage when it needs to be cleaned up or the clothes when they need to be picked up. Notice the children when they need a father's attention. And also notice her! A woman feels love and kindness when she doesn't have to always tell you what she wants. In her mind she is thinking, "if he really loved me, he would know what I want, without me having to tell him for the 100th time." Men... become more aware!

Love is also not competing with your wife. When she takes a risk, like my accountability partner did, to speak into your life; don't go tick for tack. In other words, if what she said offends you at that moment, please make yourself remember she has good intentions. She only wants your good and believes that what she is telling you will help in the long run. Take her words, without retaliating back with an offensive statement, and just meditate on them for a while. Sometimes you will come to appreciate that it was worth the initial "sting" of her words to produce a result that is much greater. Remember you two are on the same team, so stop competing against her.

Love does not say, "It's going to be my way or the highway." That's pride! God has designed us to be equal partners in the relationship. Just because a man has been given positional authority does not make him superior to his wife. We are equals and it is in that equilibrium that we will find the joy and peace we long for in our covenant relationships.

Love is being very courteous to our wives. Just remembering little things like saying "thank you" and "please" will go a long way. I can't tell you the number of times I've seen men very unknowingly show a lack of love for their wives by the little things they take for granted. Things that their wives do so routinely that the husband just takes them for granted. Don't take the little things for granted because it is the little foxes that spoil the vine.

To love your wife also means to seek to understand what her needs are, and not always be so centered on just your own needs. Whether it's her spiritual, emotional, sexual, physical or even her psychological needs, seek to understand them. As Steven Covey would say, "seek first to understand and then to be understood." Understand your wife and her needs and I can guarantee you that this one will pay big dividends over time.

Loving our wives also means that we must become quick to listen, slow to speak and slow to become angry.

"My dear brothers [and sisters], take note of this: Everyone should be quick to listen, slow to speak and slow to become angry, for man's anger does not bring about the righteous life that God desires."
James 1:19-20

A loving husband, while he sees when his wife has wronged him, doesn't keep a record book. He is not waiting to bring up the number of times he's been hurt in the past in order to win a current argument. The love this husband has for his wife is always looking for the good. So many times our minds are wired in such a way that we are listening for the bad versus thinking good thoughts about our wives. A loving husband learns how to listen to and how to trust the heart of his wife, which usually has good intentions.

I was talking to a buddy of mine and he gave me a wonderful, yet unfamiliar scripture that I'd like to share with you. In Deuteronomy 24:5, we read:

When a man has taken a new wife, he shall not go out to war or be charged with any business; he shall be free at home one year, and bring happiness to his wife whom he has taken.

Wow! What a powerful sentiment of how God would have us to love our wives. In order to bring happiness to our wives, we would first need to know what makes them happy!

We need to become students of our wives and learn about them. We need to learn what they like and what they dislike. We need to learn about their hopes and their dreams. We need to learn about what makes them unique and different from every other creature on the planet.

We also need to learn as much as we can about the "seasons" they go through every month (on their monthly cycle) and how it affects them physically, psychologically and emotionally. We also need to pay attention to how those seasons eventually affect us as men.

Learn to live in an earnest expectation of nothing but good things from your wife and your marriage and remember that... as a man thinks, so is he. Always take the position in your mind that your wife has good intentions. She only wants what's best for you.

Regardless of how it looks on the outside, make a commitment to yourself, to your wife and to God that no matter what happens, you are not going to quit. Quitting is not an option. Now that's love!

Balance in all things is going to be the key to the victory. Sometimes we learn a new truth and we take it to the extreme: either too far to the right or too far to the left. What I'm talking about doing in this chapter is to make a series of small adjustments. Let's work on a few little things and little-by-little we will find ourselves winning a major victory. Balancing our desires with the discipline to see them through is a key to the victory.

While it might not appear that you are making progress early on, remember that the journey of a thousand miles starts with the first step. But not only that, the journey also takes a consistency of continuing to take step after step after step. Although it might take a while, I can guarantee you the journey will be worth it.

Lastly, as the wife speaks "truth in respect" to her husband, it will bear fruit. The husband must learn to celebrate that. It must be celebrated both early and often. Even before the words bear fruit, start the celebration because the fruit will surely come. Remember to celebrate early and to celebrate often. As we do this, we will see an amazing thing take place. We will actually start to willingly give to our spouse what we want to receive. Let's talk about that some more in the next chapter.

$$\Omega$$

What Every Woman Needs to Hear,
What Every Man Needs to Know

Questions for Couple or Group Discussion

1. Where are one or two areas we have seen our relationship become out of balance?

2. What will we do intentionally to get balance back into our relationship?

Couple Exercise:

Use the "The Seven Steps for Resolving Disagreements" to resolve each area.

- 6 -

Part Two:
Covenant Relationship Laws

Doing Your Part

*"They shall write down days of
the year and they shall
remember them not."*

Once, Dee and I were conducting a seminar where we were teaching couples how to do Marriage Mentoring with other couples. During the seminar, a certain couple really caught our attention. They seemed to be a very nice couple; however we could tell they were really struggling in their own marriage. Throughout the time we spent with them that day, we learned their marriage had faced some very challenging times and they were both in their second marriages.

Before the couple left for the day, the wife asked Dee if she would be willing to get together with her for lunch. She went on to say something I found to be very interesting. She told Dee she wanted to get together for lunch; and her words to Dee were "not to fix me, but just to encourage one another."

Dee and I later got an invitation to dinner at their home and it was, without a doubt, one of the largest houses I had ever entered. It was obvious that they were millionaires many times over and the house was a trophy to that accomplishment. However, the thing Dee and I noticed the most was how empty the house felt. It felt almost like a kind of "death" was present inside.

While the couple had amassed all the trappings of the world; large house, fancy cars, expensive clothes and jewelry, the wife still found herself feeling empty inside and in need of encouragement. While encouragement has its place and we all need it from time to time, sometimes we need to encourage ourselves by just doing a few simple things. Little did she know but the solution to her problem was as simple as the Four (4) Laws of Covenant Relationships.

For many years, the wife had blamed most of her problems on her husband; for what he had or had not done. Her solution, in the past had always been to just go out and buy more stuff. The more stuff she got, the more encouraged she was, or at least for a while. When her husband didn't give her the love she needed, she just went out and bought more stuff until eventually she started to notice that she couldn't buy enough stuff to fill the emptiness she felt inside. No matter how much stuff she bought, she felt emptier and emptier inside until eventually she felt as if something had died inside of her.

She got expensive counseling for her problem in order to "fix" herself and while that seemed to work, it too was only a temporary fix. She would eventually find herself reverting back to old patterns. While her expensive counselors seemed to make some great suggestions on how to "fix" her dilemma, all the fixes only turned out to be short lived solutions. She constantly found herself back in that state of feeling empty, miserable and lifeless on the inside.

She had been blaming her husband for all of her problems even though she readily admitted she had not fulfilled her obligations in their relationship. Had she taken her eyes off of what her husband was or was not doing to make her life miserable and took responsibility for what she needed to do in the relationship, her whole outlook would have changed and shortly thereafter her relationship would have changed as well.

While Dee and I never got an opportunity to actually sit down and minister to that couple one-on-one, I can honestly say that she is one of the main reasons we are writing this book. Since we know we will never have the opportunity and the privilege of sitting down one-on-one with all the couples we would like to help; what follows are the things we would have done to encourage her. This represents what we have done with just about all other couples that we mentor; regarding their part in the covenant relationship.

Doing Your Part
Covenant Relationship Law #1

Each party is responsible to do what is good for the covenant relationship

In our day and time there is a very popular television show known as *CSI*. "CSI" stands for Criminal Scene Investigation. The basic premise of the show is to investigate a crime after it has already occurred to identify who the criminal is and then to put them behind bars.

In the show, they have criminal investigators who are known as profilers. The profiler's job is to basically get inside the mindset of the criminal. They try to get to what the criminal was thinking when they committed the crime. They ask lots and lots of questions because they know if they can understand the thinking of the criminal, they can ultimately solve the crime.

In a similar way we have looked at relationships and we are coining the phrase "RSI," which stands for Relationship Scene Investigation. If we were to become profilers for relationships that are either dead or are on the verge of death, we too can identify both the responsible culprit to the crime and ultimately put the criminal behind bars.

Understanding the thinking of the relationship culprit is the key. What was she thinking when she committed the relationship crime? What was he thinking when he did the "thing" that finally became the straw that broke the camel's back in their relationship? Or were they thinking at all?

After thoroughly profiling lot's of RSI's (Relationship Scene Investigations), we have identified six main reasons or culprits for most of the relationships that we have seen to go wrong. In an effort to put a positive spin on it, we have reversed our thinking to come up with some ingredients that would have saved their relationship.

What follows are six ideas we would have had them to think about. We believe an idea is sometimes all it takes to avoid having a RSI. We are calling these ideas the Six (6) Habits of Healthy Relationships.

63

Six Habits of Healthy Relationships

1. Work on the covenant relationship by spending time together

2. Learn how to hear "the voice" behind the voice of your covenant partner

3. Learn and understand "your" role in the covenant relationship

4. Give respect where respect is due

5. Give love where love is due

6. Live out of covenant relationship; not out of thoughts and emotions

Spending Time Together

Absolutely nothing will replace spending time together in covenant relationship. This is by far the number one ingredient to happy and successful relationships. This is the main thing; the first in importance; the principle thing or whatever adjectives we need to use to get the point across. This is it! Our first and foremost covenant relationship is with God and the more time we spend with Him the better our relationships are both with Him and others.

We have found every couple has a "best" time to communicate. In other words, we have a "best" time for us to hear one another. As an example, I am not a very good listener late at night. My body usually starts to shut down around 8 or 9 o'clock at night, so my wife and I have found that late nights are not a good time for us to spend quality time together communicating; especially if we need to have some important discussion.

Since I am an early-to-bed kind of guy, I am also usually up very early in the morning. A typical wake up time for me is around 3a.m. or so. I will usually spend hours in prayer, studying, meditating or just having some quiet time. Dee, on the other hand is usually a very light sleeper. When she hears me up and about, and she has something on her heart or mind, she will usually get up and express herself.

Likewise, we have found that 6a.m. to 8a.m. are not hours that fit in really good with my wife's demeanor. She is normally really busy getting ready for the day concentrating on all that needs to be done both for our family and herself. She is very focused on making sure we all get what we need and she is not really open to a deep soul searching conversation.

Having said all this, what we have found to be our "best" time to spend quality time together communicating is around 4a.m. in the morning. Now before you get alarmed, please know I am not recommending that 4a.m. in the morning will work best for everyone. I'm just saying that is what we found to work best for us. All couples must find their own "best" time to communicate based on their particular nuances, temperaments and circumstances.

What we have found, and it has proven to be true for us, time and time again, is that 4a.m. is an ideal time for us to spend quality time together in productive communication. We both seem to "hear" each other best early in the morning. While 4a.m. may or may not work for you, it is important to find a time you and your spouse can spend some quality time together in some very meaningful discussion.

Whether you're having a conversation, just drinking a cup of coffee together, enjoying a movie or going for a walk in the park; NOTHING will replace spending time together. It is the number one ingredient in the recipe for happy and prosperous relationships.

Hear "the Voice" Behind the Voice

Many times I have asked my wife, "How are you doing, honey?" and the response I will get is "I'm okay." Since we spend so much time together I know when okay means, okay! Sometimes her "okay" means, if you really loved me, you would know what's going on with me. We must learn to hear the voice behind the voice of our covenant partner.

We were once mentoring a couple and it seemed as if the time we were spending with them was producing no results. I found myself becoming very frustrated with the couple. I remember saying, Lord I know you have called us to this ministry, but it seems as if we are getting nowhere. God, in his typically response reminded me of how patient He, and others, had been with me.

Shortly after that discussion with God, I was being led to have a different type of mentoring session with the couple we were mentoring. Instead of our usual session where we would normally sit across the table from each other as couples and have some very lengthy conversations; this time we would do things a little differently. We invited them to our home for dinner; we had a glass of wine and then played a leisurely game of cards together.

After just a short while, it became very apparent to all of us that John (which is the name we will use for the male in the relationship) was a very good card player. In fact, John was so good that the couple won several games straight against us. John seemed to always know which cards to play and even found himself coaching his wife-to-be along the way. Then it dawned on me! The same way John had become proficient at this game of cards is the exact same way he would learn to hear "the voice" behind the voice of his soon to be covenant partner. John had studied the game. He had learned the game by both playing it many, many times and by becoming a student of the game.

Likewise, he must now become a student of his wife-to-be. He must spend time with her and learn her likes and dislikes; what makes her happy and what makes her sad; what gives her energy and what seems to drain the life out of her; what fuels her dreams and what keeps her awake at night worrying. It was time for John to become a student of his wife-to-be and learn how to hear "the voice" behind the voice.

John did just that and they found the breakthrough they were seeking. And the good news is, it didn't take very long. In just a few short weeks we could see a profound difference in their relationship.

We eventually married that couple and they are currently doing great! That one simple change has carried on in their relationship allowing them not only to enjoy one another but also to become a model of what can happen if we are only willing to take the time to learn how to hear "the voice" behind the voice or our covenant partner.

Understand Your Role

This is without question one of the most important factors in the building and sustaining of strong covenant relationships. Identifying, understanding and fulfilling your role in the covenant relationship is the key to the victory. I am 100% responsible for my role in the covenant relationship and not for my spouse's role. Please, don't miss that! I am 100% responsible to do what God told me to do in the covenant relationship and not for what He told my wife to do in our relationship.

So many times we tend to look outward, as individuals, versus looking inward. What I am saying is that most of the time when a couple comes in for counseling for the first time, it is ALWAYS the other persons fault. They tend to see all the wrong their spouse is doing, but can in no way see fault in them self.

In Matthew 7:5, we hear:

> You hypocrite, first take the plank out of your own eye, and then you will see clearly to remove the speck from your brother's eye.

The word clearly means to recover full vision or to look through. In other words, once we take the responsibility to do our part in the covenant relationship, we take out the obstacles that would our vision. We can see clearly and have full vision in order to see through the tricks of the enemy. We help our covenant partner to see clearly only after we get full vision ourselves.

When we are not doing our part; we are not seeing clearly or we are not seeing with full vision. You won't believe the number of times folks have come to see us who are currently in the middle of an adulterous relationship and want us to help them "fix" their covenant partner. They are not seeing correctly and that's a fact.

On one occasion, it is recorded that Jesus said these words... "While seeing they don't see." What he is referring to is that while we have our physical ability to see, we really are not able to discern or to see what is really going on. When we do our part in the covenant relationship, we regain our ability to see clearly and many obstacles will be avoided; especially in the areas of communication and conflict resolution.

Some might ask, "What are our roles?" Especially now-a-days when we have so many couples where both spouses work outside the home. What's most important is to make sure you communicate and come to some agreement on who's going to do what. Agree on both roles and responsibilities.

As you agree on your roles and responsibilities, you will find that living life in covenant relationship becomes much easier and much more satisfying. Coming to agreement is the key and we will talk in much more detail about this later. Now let's take a look at what could be our most important role in covenant relationships.

Give what is DUE ...not Earned!
(Love & Respect)

Ephesians 5:33 says:

> However, each one of you must love his wife as he loves himself, and the wife must respect her husband.

The word *must* here is used to mean it is absolutely necessary. It is necessary a husband love his wife and it is necessary that a wife respect her husband. It is a necessary thing for a wife to receive love. It is of utmost necessity for a man to receive respect. God wired us in such a way that those things are a need, not a want. That's why they are DUE and don't have to be earned.

The word *due* means owed immediately. We owe each other that which God commanded us to give. God did not tell the wife to love her husband, because she has been internally programmed in such a way that she does that automatically. The good Lord did not tell a husband to respect his wife because what she needs most is his love. God wired her that way.

At the core of just about every disagreement we have uncovered in our own relationship and in the relationships we have had an opportunity to minister to are these two fundamental issues; Love and Respect. When a woman doesn't feel loved, she responds disrespectfully. When a man feels as though he is not being respected, he responds in an unloving way. They seem to go hand in hand.

Therefore remember, men, to give love to your spouse because you owe it to her, whether she has earned it or not. It is due and does not have to be earned. Likewise, women, give respect to your husband because you owe it to him. It is due and does not need to be earned. That's Gods way of doing things and it will never fail.

Live out of Covenant Relationship

To live out of covenant relationship and not out of thoughts and emotions is a form of discipline. So often we have been conditioned as men to believe that we are "thinkers" and we should allow our thoughts to guide us. While that may sound good, I don't have to tell you your thoughts can guide you to some very unwanted and unholy places. In fact, the Bible teaches us to take our thoughts captive and make them obedient to Christ. In other words, we should guide our thoughts and not allow our thoughts to just have free reign over our lives.

The following scripture has been a life changing passage for me. Romans 12:2, says:

> Do not conform any longer to the pattern of this world, but be transformed by the renewing of your mind. Then you will be able to test and approve what God's will is–his good, pleasing and perfect will.

We must renew our minds to the Word of God. We must change our thinking to make it line up with God's way of thinking. When we find out what God has to say on a particular subject, we must then allow the Spirit of God, who lives inside of us, to guide us. Finally we must take the coordinating action. We are then being transformed. Again, it works like this:

1. The word of God informs us
2. The Spirit of God guides us
3. The children of God take the actions

When we follow these three simple steps, not only will we know what God's good, pleasing, and perfect will is; but will also do his will. And that's where the blessing is found. It's in the doing. Check out the following passage found in James 1:22:

Do not merely listen to the word and so deceive yourselves. Do what it says.

This is such a true statement. The drug addict knows he's a drug addict; he just won't do anything about it. The alcoholic knows he is an alcoholic, but just won't do what it takes to conquer the addiction. The list goes on and on and relationships are no different. The person in a wrong relationship knows it! They just won't do what it takes to change their situation to either get out or make it better.

Just like so many men have been conditioned to believe they are "thinkers", in a similar way, many women have been conditioned to believe they are "emotional" beings and as such should make decisions based on how they feel. This is equally as dangerous because we are not what we feel.

Our feelings change and they change…**all the time**! If we were to make our decisions based on feelings, alone, we would make a mess of things all day long. Our feelings truly can mislead us. The passage below in Isaiah shows us that our feelings are not always the best of guides. It reads:

Like the blind we grope along the wall, feeling our way like men without eyes. At midday we stumble as if it were twilight; among the strong, we are like the dead.
- Isaiah 59:10

To live out of covenant relationship is to live the way God intended for us. In the past we have all conformed to the patterns of this world. Or in other words, we have created patterns in our lives based on the world's way of doing things. The television shows we watch and the music we listen to wants to condition our thoughts, emotions and ultimately our actions.

The world wants to tell us how to handle our children, how to manage our money, what clothes to wear and what type of car to drive. The world wants to influence us on what to eat, what to drink, what to think, and the list goes on and on and on. The passage in Romans 12:2 is asking us to re-evaluate the way we have been thinking and ultimately the way we have been living. It challenges us to look at a different way of thinking; God's way of thinking.

Again, when we renew our mind to God's way of thinking, we will not only be changed, but we will know what God's good, pleasing, and perfect will is for our lives. I can tell you without any reservation that God wants us to have happy and productive covenant relationships, first with Him and then with one another. God wants our marriages to be so loving and so kind that people see us and want to know the secret of our relationship success. We have become ONE and although that is a mystery to some, I believe that God is allowing us to understand that mystery more and more. It starts with our covenant relationship, first to God and then to one another.

God is now, and has always been, a covenant keeping God. In fact, we have been made in God's image and in His likeness and we too should be covenant keeping people. One of the most important covenants known to man is a covenant between a husband and wife. In Genesis 2:24, we read:

> For this reason a man will leave his father and mother and be united to his wife, and they will become one flesh.

I believe the reason for this is very simple. God wants to do something in and through us that He can only do with covenant people.

In a covenant relationship with our spouse, God changes our thinking and our emotions to the point where we truly become one flesh. We care so deeply for one another that we begin to put the interest of each other before our very own. We begin to live out of covenant relationship and not out of thoughts, emotions, selfishness or vain glory. We become the people of God that we were sent here to be.

As we continually renew our minds to God's way of doing things, we find the rewards are incredible as we'll now see in Covenant Relationship Law #2.

Ω

What Every Woman Needs to Hear,
What Every Man Needs to Know

Questions for Couple or Group Discussion

1. What is my part in the covenant relationship?

2. Review the "Six Habits of Healthy Relationships" and fill in the blank.

"I will do what is good for my covenant relationship by
_____ "

- 7 -

It's A Matter of Life & Death

Covenant Relationship Law #2

To keep the covenant agreement is rewardable by entering into the Life Cycle; and to break the covenant agreement is punishable by entering into the Death Cycle.

Since we will spend a considerable amount of time in this chapter discussing both the Life Cycle and the Death Cycle, I think it's important to give a definition of the Life Cycle right up front. In a nutshell, the Life Cycle consists of things like love, joy, peace, security, well-being, happiness, friendliness, health, prosperity, patience, kindness, goodness, faithfulness, gentleness and the ability to control our thoughts and emotions.

At first glance this might seem impossible to achieve, however, I believe that God's plan for us is to achieve this through covenant relationships. It's up to us to learn (by continually renewing our minds) God's way of thinking. Let's get started.

The word *law* has been defined for our purposes as an established principle that works the same way, all the time. For instance, the law of gravity will work the same way all the time. What goes up must come down.

The law of the seedtime and harvest works the same way all the time. If you plant an apple seed, you will get an apple. If you plant an orange seed, it will most definitely produce an orange. We can cross-breed dogs until we are blue in the face and we will still produce a dog. It might be a big dog, a short dog, a spotted dog, a curly-hair dog, a white dog or a long legged dog – but the result is the same. It's a dog. The law of seedtime and harvest works the same way all the time. Whatever we plant is what we will eventually harvest.

Likewise, in Covenant Relationship Law #2, we have two laws that are always in operation as it pertains to both our living and our relationships. As we learn to work in these laws effectively, they will begin to work effectively in our relationships.

In Romans 8:2 we read:

...through Christ Jesus the law of the Spirit of life set me free from the law of sin and death.

Let's go back to an earlier example of the wife that lived in the very expensive home and had all the things that money could buy. While it looked as if things were going extremely well for her, she was dying inside and couldn't figure out why. She had gone to expensive doctors and therapists and all they advised her to do only would work for a little while. They were all just temporary fixes. She longed for a solution to her problem, but it seemed that no one could help her.

While Dee and I never got an opportunity to minister to her, we have had the opportunity to reach many others in similar situations. Had we been given the opportunity to minister to her, we would have shared with her the Four Law's of Covenant Relationship. Since we know we will never be able to minister to all the couples that we would like to on a one-to-one basis, we have committed our thoughts to writing. They have been such an inspiration and help to countless others.

Once you hear the Four Laws of Covenant Relationship and begin to apply the principles in your own relationship, the Life Cycle will be induced. When the wife fulfills her role in the covenant relationship, whether her husband deserves it or not, the Life Cycle continues. When she respects his position as the head of the house and also as a man, it brings marvelous results. The death that she was feeling on the inside will slowly begin to dissipate and she will sense life coming into both herself and into her relationship. What's happening? She is turning on the Life Cycle by her willingness to keep the covenant agreement.

So likewise, when a husband is willing to do his part and takes 100% responsibility for doing it, he is turning on the Life Cycle by his willingness to keep the covenant agreement.

There is so much power in agreement. When couples can agree they are virtually unstoppable. The bible says that a house divided cannot stand. We are also told that when we can agree, God will be in the middle of our agreement. In Matthew 18:19, we read:

> Again, I tell you that if two of you on earth agree about anything you ask for, it will be done for you by my Father in heaven.

I can remember getting a call late one Sunday evening from a couple, beckoning my wife and me to come to their home. They had just been in a heated argument and the wife asked her husband to leave the home. Well, asking is actually putting it mildly. She had basically insisted that he leave immediately.

After Dee and I assessed the situation, we knew that they were both taking a selfish position. The couple had been married for less than two years and they both had children from previous marriages. On this particular occasion they had argued over something small and then it escalated into something about the kids. At this point the wife had just about all that she could take and insisted they either separate until they could iron out their differences or she wanted a divorce.

Once we had some time to calm them both down; we searched for areas they could agree on. They agreed that they loved each other and were both willing to work on their relationship. After about an hour or so we had come up with a written agreement that allowed the husband to remain in his home for the next two weeks. He would sleep in the guest bedroom and they would continue to share household responsibilities.

They also worked out a schedule in which they agreed to communicate on a daily basis. They agreed to use a book on relationships to guide their discussion. They agreed to have no sexual contact for those two weeks, but to create other ways to have intimacy if they so chose to. After all was said and done, they had about ten items on the page that they both could agree to. They both signed the agreement and I also signed as a witness.

The last item on the agreement was to come back together in two weeks to track their progress. When we met at the end of that two week period, we were amazed at the progress the coupled had made. That was the last mentoring session Dee and I had with that couple. I am glad to report they are doing well and their relationship has prospered. Agreement was the key. They just didn't know how to sit down as a couple and come to agreement.

While I debated about sharing this point, I think it's important to note that, as for this couple, they were both leaders in their local church. I only point this out because there might be some pastor or leader in a church saying "where do I go for help?" or even worse, "should I seek help"? Please believe me when I say that help is available and the bible teaches us very clearly that we should seek wise counsel. If you cannot find competent and confidential help in your area, please contact DEDAN Ministry to Marriages at dedan.org. Through the work we have done with marriages, we have contacts virtually worldwide we can direct you to. Your situation will be treated with respect, kindness, care, and with the utmost in confidentiality. Now let's continue.

Even when couples disagree, if they can learn to do it agreeably, they still have the victory. Life is found in agreement. The Life Cycle is found when couples can learn to agree. Dee and I have found that when couples can't see eye to eye, if we can find at least one thing they will agree on, we know we are working with agreeable people. And when we are working with agreeable people, the Life Cycle will surely follow.

The Life Cycle is that place where you find contentment. It is mostly an inner contentment and has little to do with the outside circumstances of your life. It's that place where you have decided to be the best that you can be regardless of the decision that anyone else makes. You make a decision to live and not die. You make a decision to walk in the Spirit and not fulfill the desires of the flesh.

When someone is being rude or unkind to you, the easiest decision to make is to be rude and unkind to them. But that only exasperates the situation. When we add oil to a fire we just get a bigger fire. When we exchange hate for hate, we just get more of the same. However, when we show respect to a husband, even when there is an absence of love on his part, we turn on the Life

Cycle. As a husband, when we show love to our wives, even in the absence of respect, we too turn on the Life Cycle.

Check out the following quote by Roger Merrill:

> The Life is within the seed.

The brevity of this quote almost takes away the enormous insight that it reveals. In Genesis 1:12, we see this same sentiment:

> The land produced vegetation: plants bearing seed according to their kinds and trees bearing fruit with seed in it according to their kinds. And God saw that it was good.

When I plant a seed of love into my wife's life, I turn on the Life Cycle because the "seed" that I planted has life in it and it will produce after its own kind. The more love I show to my wife, the more seeds I plant with life inside of them. The more seeds I plant with life inside of them, the greater the harvest. God's word is true and it will never return to Him void, but will accomplish what He sent it to do. I will paraphrase Isaiah 55:11, when God says:

> The word that goes out from my mouth will not return to me empty, but will accomplish what I desire and achieve the purpose for which I sent it.

My wife Dee is a master at this. Before I grabbed on to these principles and began to apply them into my own life and relationships, my wife was already there.

Early in our marriage, I can remember coming home tired some nights from a long day at work and I would find myself becoming easily frustrated. I mean any little thing could throw me off the deep end. It could be that dinner was not ready or maybe Dee wanted to have a conversation and I wasn't in the mood or it could be something as simple as what we were watching on television. But I noticed something about my wife. She would always respect me, no matter how I reacted towards her.

I can remember on several occasions her making the comment, "you're just tired, why don't you get some rest." Little did I know

77

at the time, but she was planting seeds of life that would eventually produce after its own kind.

I can now judge myself and I know when I'm tired I can become easily frustrated. Therefore, out of the love I have for Dee and the sense of always wanting to show her that love, I find myself, "checking" myself. If I feel as though I am about to become annoyed or frustrated, I will lovingly ask to be excused so I can get some rest or I will ask if we can have the conversation at another time.

I also find myself being very sensitive to the needs of my wife and on many occasions putting her needs above my own. I believe with all my heart that this is a direct result of all the years that my wife planted the seeds of life (respect) into my life. Now she is reaping the harvest of love.

Unfortunately however the Death Cycle works in the exact same way. Have you ever noticed that things seem to be going great and all of the sudden you find yourself in a disagreement with your spouse, significant other or it could be anyone you're in a covenant relationship with? It could be a boss, a child, a co-worker – and the list goes on and on. Do you find yourself starting to feel drained, as if the very life is being sucked right out of you? That is called the Death Cycle and we enter into it by our own actions. Let me give you an example of what I'm saying.

In the movie, Fireproof, Caleb (played by actor Kirk Cameron) is a fireman that is in a very troubled marriage with his wife, Katherine. They get into an argument and Katherine calls Caleb selfish and self-centered. She says all he cares about is saving money for a stupid boat and pleasing himself by looking at trash [pornography] on the internet. How many of you know that the truth hurts? Anyway, Caleb is now as mad as the dickens and he lashed back with the following statement:

> You selfish and ungrateful woman. You show me no respect. All you do is nag and complain. You drain the life out of me.

The statement that I would like to draw your attention to is the last one. "You drain the life out of me." This is such a profound and true statement. It seems as if the very life that is within us is being sucked right out of us when we are constantly in disagreement in our relationships. Whether it's a disagreement with a spouse, a boss at work, a co-worker or one of your children, conflicts and disagreements just seem to suck the very life out of us.

That is the reason why understanding Covenant Relationship Law #2 is so very important. To keep the covenant agreement is rewardable by entering into the Life Cycle; and to break the covenant agreement is punishable by entering into the Death Cycle.

When we keep the covenant agreement, by doing our part, we plant seeds of life and when we break the covenant agreement, by entering into our selfish and self-centered nature, we plant seeds of death. It is as simple as that and just remember when all else fails, go back to Covenant Relationship Law #1.

Ω

What Every Woman Needs to Hear,
What Every Man Needs to Know

Questions for Couple or Group Discussion

1. When was a time recently in our relationship where we experienced the death cycle?

2. What did we do specifically to get out of the death cycle?

3. When was a time recently in our relationship where we experienced the life cycle?

4. Are we in the life cycle now? If not what are one or two things we can do specifically to get back on track?

Defending Against "The Threat"

Covenant Relationship Law #3

When we do our part in the covenant relationship, we defend against "the threat."

There is always a threat against our relationships. Division or disagreement is one of the #1 weapons of the enemy. We have been told countless times that a house divided cannot stand or what about the following very important passage:

> The thief comes only to steal and kill and destroy; I have come that you may have life, and have it to the full.

Here we see very clearly that we do have an enemy we call "the thief." Secondly, we see the thief has a job to do; which is to steal and kill and destroy our relationships. The threat to our relationship is that thief. While the thief has been known to show up in many ways, we would like to show you a very familiar pattern we have seen.

Trust, Disappointment and Re-defining Relationships

I got a call one afternoon from a buddy of mine and he started the conversation by saying, "I need your help!" Right away I dropped everything I was doing and I centered my full attention on him. This is the kind of guy that rarely asked for help, so I knew something major was going on.

My buddy, who we will call Tom for our purposes, goes on to tell me that one of his best friends and accountability partner just called him and said he was ready to leave his wife. The friend asked Tom for some guidance, but Tom didn't know what to tell him. However, Tom assured him that he would reach out to someone for advice and call him back. Here's the skinny:

Tom's friend and his wife had been having problems communicating in the area of their finances. The husband was a stickler for a budget and the wife seemed to always overspend her allocated monthly funds. If I remember correctly, the wife had a budget of $1,500 a month and she would regularly spend over $2,000 a month. After several very unpleasant conversations about her overspending, the husband thought they had come to an agreement on the matter and that his wife would try to do better.

A few months later however, the husband was checking the balances of their bank accounts online and he noticed a $5,000 withdrawal had been transferred from their joint checking account into the wife's checking account that she used for her monthly budget. After a "brief" cooling down period, the husband called his wife on the phone and asked her why she had moved the $5,000 to her account. His wife responded, "I was just getting sick and tired of always having to come to you and ask for money." After a few very heated exchanges of words, the husband backed down and said, to himself, "that's it, I'm leaving."

Fortunately, before the husband packed his bags and hit the door, he took the time to call my friend Tom and ask for advice. Tom had known this guy for many years and had spent countless hours on the phone with him as they journeyed through life together. They had been accountability partners for many years, but Tom had never seen his friend react this way towards his wife, nor had his friend ever, in all those years, threatened to leave his wife.

The husband and wife had been married for over twenty years and they had two wonderful kids. They lived in a very expensive home and they were both good Church-going folks. So what's the rub? Why such a sense of urgency about leaving now and especially over something as miniscule as money?

> What causes fights and quarrels among you? Don't they come from your desires that battle within you?
>
> - James 4:1

Think about the question, "What causes fights and quarrels among you?" The Bible tells us that the quarrels and the fights come from some desire you have on the inside of you that just won't let you have peace. Nine times out of ten, when there is a rub in a relationship, we find out that the "stated" issue is not the real issue. There is something underlying that is the real issue. And it is always that underlying issue that is the real "threat" to the relationship.

When my buddy Tom explained the situation to me, I immediately told him the issue was not money. Anyone that could move $5,000 around like that and it go unnoticed for even a little while is truly not in a pinch for money. The true threat to their relationship was this issue of trust, disappointment and a need to redefine their relationship.

Trust

The husband had lost his trust in his wife and the wife had lost her trust in her husband. If fact, if truth be told, when they made the last agreement to budget more effectively, something deep inside of the husband was just waiting to see how long it would take for his wife to break the agreement this time. He was probably "unintentionally" monitoring the bank accounts in an effort to see just how long it would take for her to go back to her familiar pattern of overspending.

So likewise, when the wife made the agreement she probably had good "intentions" but since she could feel the husbands mistrust, it lead to a similar mistrust in his ability to meet her needs. In fact, she really didn't trust that he even had a desire to meet her needs fully. All he cared about, in her mind, was the budget.

The wife's mistrust then led to that old familiar feeling of disappointment. When the wife moved the money, the husband then felt that same old, but very familiar, feeling of disappointment also. When that feeling hit him, he acted almost instinctively in a very unloving way. When he went into an instinctive reaction, it represented an old familiar pattern to his wife and lead to a similar old but very familiar reaction of disrespect towards him. Here we go again with the same old stuff! New day, same old mess.

Disappointment

The word disappointment has a very interesting dual meaning. It means:

1. To fail to fulfill the expectations or wishes of
2. To defeat the fulfillment of (hopes, plans, etc.); to thwart; frustrate

On the one hand, the wife failed to fulfill the expectations of the new budget agreement they had made. However, the second definition is the one that is of the most concern. The disappointment they both experienced, seemingly, over such a small thing as money, was about to defeat the fulfillment of their hopes and plans to be wedded for life. They had both become frustrated with one another and that frustration almost thwarted their plans to be husband and wife until death do they part.

What could cause such a deep frustration, lack of trust and disappointment as to bring up such a permanent solution [divorce] for such a temporary problem [money]? What could cause the husband to get to the point where he would actually call a friend and say I am about to give up, cave in and quit on my marriage?

You see, deep down inside, the husband had a desire within him for his wife's respect and when he felt that he was not getting that, he instinctively responded in a way that she viewed as unloving. So likewise, the wife had a deep desire within her for her husband's love and when she felt as though he wasn't giving her that, she responded in a way that he viewed as totally disrespectful.

When the husband was viewed as behaving un-lovingly and the wife was viewed as behaving disrespectfully, they both failed to realize what was needed at the time was a redefinition of their relationship. They had been working off of an old relationship map and it was time to sit down and talk about some changes that had taken place in their relationship landscape over time.

Redefining Relationships

The easiest way for me to explain this principle is as follows. The girl named Dee that I met in college and eventually fell in love with is not the young lady I married. The young lady I married on December 22, 1984 is not the woman who gave birth to our first child, Dierdre. The woman who gave birth to our first child, Dierdre, is not the same woman who eventually became a nurse and went out into the work world. The person who went out into the work world, as a nurse, is not the same person who bore our second daughter, Danielle. The person who bore Danielle is not the same lady that helped me start a church and multiple businesses and eventually the ministry to marriages we currently enjoy.

In other words, the message we want to convey here is… people change over time. Hopefully that change is filled with growth and productivity, but regardless, change happens. Therefore, since change is inevitable we must stop from time to time in our relationships and ask the question, "who are we now?"

Once we see that we have changed and hopefully grown in a certain area, we can then take on new authority in that area and new responsibility. When we grow and change in our relationship, it's time to redefine our relationship.

For example, Dee and I had a season in our life where Dee could stay at home with the children while they were young, as a house mom. I was making a substantial income at that time and my job was to work outside of the home while Dee worked inside. During that season of our life, we looked a lot like a traditional family in our roles and responsibilities. However, something changed.

We gradually went into a season where I had been called out of corporate America and into full time ministry. During that transition, Dee would sometimes work a full time job as a school nurse and a part time job on weekends in order to help us make ends meet. While Dee was working outside the house, I began to work more inside the home.

This was a major shift for us and required lots of communication and sacrifice. In other words, we had to redefine our relationship. This is one of the most misunderstood principles in relationships. When circumstances and situations in our lives change, we must adapt to the situation, make changes where necessary and then just go with the flow.

Just to close out the story on the couple in the earlier example, I am glad to tell you they had a happy ending. Once they could see that their relationship landscape had changed, they agreed to sit down again and have a heart-to-heart discussion. This time as opposed to just focusing on a budget, they discussed area's in their relationship that dealt with trust, disappointment and where redefining their relationship could help.

They agreed that they had both changed and grown substantially in the area of finances. They agreed to make some changes in their approach to budgeting and money management that gave the wife more authority for decision making within a reasonable framework. They also agreed that if any changes to their plan were necessary, over an agreed upon amount, the wife had the responsibility to bring those changes back to the table for discussion so they could come to agreement together.

While they had come to agreement and also come up with a plan, what would be different about it this time? They had come to agreement and had come up with plans in the past, so what would be different about this time? This time there was one fundamental difference.

This time they redefined their relationship by seeing from the perspective of the other. The wife knew that her keeping the agreement was a way to both earn her husband's trust, while at the same time showing him the respect he so greatly desires.

So likewise, the husband knew that his agreeing to his wife to having more authority and responsibility in decisions about their finances would show he trusted her financial decision making ability. It would also show her kindness by letting her know that he had not lost hope in her. All of which are fruits of love and love never fails.

Guarding Against "The Threat"

While there is absolutely no way that we have found to stop the threat from coming, we can stop the threat from overcoming. In fact, we can very effectively guard against the threat when we understand the inward needs of our covenant partner and then work consistently to meet those needs.

It is truly not our intent to claim this list includes all the needs of women and men. It is rather our hope to convey some of the most important needs that we have found over the years as we've met with hundreds of couples. We also did not want to give a list that was so long and exhaustive that the essence of what we are trying to accomplish gets lost. The list is short and sweet and to the point.

For women we will discuss four of the most universal needs that we have found along with an easy to remember acronym: RIBS. For the men we only discuss three universal needs and the acronym is RAS.

Four (4) Inward Needs of A Woman (RIBS)

The Bible tells us that God caused the man to fall into a deep sleep; and while he was sleeping, He took one of the man's ribs and closed up the place with flesh. Then the Lord God made a woman from the rib He had taken out of the man, and He brought her to the man. Within this one word, RIBS, a man can find the answer to that question many women ask without ever saying a word, which is basically, "Can you see me?"

Right-Relationship

The "R" stands for right-relationship. A right-relationship, as defined in scripture, is all about love. In fact, Jesus was once asked the question, "What is the greatest of all the commandments?" He responded, love!

> Love the Lord your God with all your heart and with all your soul and with all your mind. This is the first and greatest commandment. And the second is like it: "Love your neighbor as yourself."
> - Matthew 22:37-38

87

And to a husband, I believe Jesus would say:

And the second is like it: "Love your [wife] as you love yourself."

As a matter of record, God did give men that very commandment in Ephesians 5:33, when he says, through Paul, each one of you also must love his wife as he loves himself, and the wife must respect her husband.

Love is by far the greatest inward need of every woman. God designed her that way and nothing else will do. Nothing else can even compare to love. When a woman feels loved, it's as if she is in the very presence of God. And in fact, she is, because God is love.

Romance is also very important as men function in their love role. Romance is not sex; however, it will lead to some great sex. Romance is all the little things that men are supposed to do that will lead to some awesome intimacy. Things like remembering those special days such as birthdays, anniversaries or Valentine day. While these examples are not as romantic as they are obligatory, they are still a must to remember.

Men also need to find more unexpected and personal things to do like keeping her gas tank full, keeping her car clean, doing chores for her or maybe giving small gifts from time to time for absolutely no reason at all. Women also view intimacy as all the little things that we do all day long such as help around the home, or helping with the children. Remembering to lower the toilet seat is on her list as well, believe it or not.

She wants romance prior to sex and there are so many little things that we can do which will go a long way in the bedroom. Listening to her and ultimately hearing what she says is very sexy to a woman. Not only that, but also knowing how, when and where to speak to your spouse will also go a long way towards intimacy. Dee often tells me, "It's not what you say, but how you say it."

In his book entitled, "Naked And Unashamed: The Journey Toward Sexual Fulfillment in Christian Marriage", Dr. Stacey L. Spencer makes the following statement:

It is easy for the line to be blurred when it comes to spirituality versus sensuality. A healthy relationship has a good blend of both. Often the distinction is forced by observers who are not in *right relationship* with God and are uncomfortable with their own nakedness. Michal, David's estranged wife, was bitter because David had forced himself back into her life after years of separation. When there is emotional separation between a man and a woman it is hard for them to connect and appreciate being uncovered.

As men, one of our number one tasks should be to learn and understand the emotional psyche of a woman. Understanding and appreciating her passions and desires is the key to connecting with her emotionally and I can tell you from many years of experience that connecting with her emotionally will open her up sensually.

Influence Authority

A woman wants to know that she is important to a man and has influence in his life. This is one of the most important factors in helping to meet the emotional need in a woman's life. When a man doesn't make her feel as though she has influence in his life, she will eventually let him know.

I heard a story once about a great president of one of the largest corporations in the world. He was on vacation with his wife of over forty years and they decided to visit the hometown they had both grown up in. When they stopped at a local gas station, they saw a guy she had dated when she was in high school. He was pumping their gas. After a few cordial exchanges with the gas attendant, the president and his wife were back on the road.

Feeling quite proud about himself and what he had accomplished in life, compared to her old boyfriend, the president said to his wife, "I bet you're pretty glad now that you married me instead of that guy, aren't you?" Without blinking an eye, his wife replied, "not really because if I had married him, he would be president and you would have been pumping our gas!"

A woman wants to know she is important to her man and that she has influence in her man's life. When he doesn't make her feel that way, she will eventually let him know.

Beauty

You have probably heard it said that beauty is only skin deep or that beauty is in the eye of the beholder. To a woman, beauty is everything. She wants to know that she is the apple in her man's eye. She wants to know she is the cream in his coffee and the only one that floats his boat. She wants to know that he is attracted to her both inside and out.

If we were to just stop and think about it for a moment, this one should be a no brainer. A woman will spend hours at a beauty shop getting her hair done at a cost each month that would probable pay for a new truck. She will get her nails done, her toes done and then go shopping all day long for that extra special attire for that special or non-special occasion. And you better notice it!!!

Tell her how beautiful she is to you. Tell her with words! Tell her with your eyes. Tell her with your actions. Tell her in front of others just how lovely she is. Please hear what I am saying to you. I am not asking you to be manipulative in any way. If she is beautiful in your eyes, then let her know. She needs to know and if you don't tell her, believe me, someone else will and her ears will want to hear it.

Dee is the apple of my eye and I let her know it in as many ways as I can think of. She knows that I believe she is beautiful both inside and out.

Security

Risk avoidance has never been one of my strong suites. I am a risk taker, pure and simple. On the other hand, Dee is not. She likes to play it safe and the fewer risks, the better in her opinion. Now those are descriptions of our individual characteristics and not meant to be a universal descriptor of men and women; however, we have noticed something about women which appears to be very universal in nature. They have a need for security.

Dee wants to know that all the bills are going to be paid and paid on time. She wants to know that if one of the children gets injured, we have insurance coverage to ensure they will be provided for. Dee wants the security of knowing that if something were to happen to me, the family would have enough life insurance coverage to maintain our current standard of living.

Dee wants the security of knowing that everything is going to be ok. While it is not totally within my power to make sure that all is well, I need to make sure that Dee has a certain degree of confidence that we are secure. I believe that our primary security rests in the fact that we know and believe in God. That security needs to be evident in my life by the consistent actions that I take.

I was once told by a pastor friend when I was going through a tough time financially to "pray like everything depended on God, and work like everything depended on me." While those were the exact words that I needed to hear at the time, I have since come to a greater understanding of both who God is and how he wants to work in our lives.

While in my study and meditation time one morning, I heard the words pray, prepare and pay attention. For me, these three words lead to security. As I make prayer a consistent part of my life, it seems that I am always preparing for the right opportunities in life. As I find myself more prepared for the opportunities my only task then is to pay attention. When the right opportunities present themselves, I'm ready!

When preparation meets opportunity it equals success.
- Author unknown

As we enjoy more of the successes in life that feeling of security is met in Dee's life. We both get to enjoy the fruits of our labor, while resting secure in the confidence that if we pray, prepare and pay attention, God will always lead us in the right direction.

The (3) Primary Needs of Men (RAS)

Respect

I almost feel like we're beating a dead horse on this one; however, we can't restate it enough. With respect a man will climb just about any mountain for you and won't get as exhausted doing it. Without respect, sometimes it hard to even get him off the couch and away from that football game he's watching on television.

Respect is the one common denominator that we see in ALL great marriages. When the wife respects her husband, even when he doesn't necessarily always deserve it, he seems to eventually come around. While it's definitely not always easy, it does seem to always pay big dividends.

One synonym for respect is admiration. When a man knows that he is admired by his covenant partner, it brings on a whole new attitude. His confidence is higher and his faith is stronger. His sense of worth is higher and in turn he works even harder to be the person that his wife so admires. Remember, we reap what we sow; therefore, sow respect into his life. Again, I know it's not always easy, but it will pay off in the end.

Affirmation

The verb affirmation comes from the root word affirm which when we search for definitions, means:

1. To state or assert positively; maintain as true
2. To express agreement with or commitment to; uphold; support
3. To make steady, strengthen
4. "Answering YES"

Supporting words of encouragement and affirmation are like the sound of music to a man's ears. A man needs to know that you are proud of him. I can't say this enough. This is the ultimate in respect for a man, just to know that you believe in him and are proud of him and his accomplishments in life.

When you notice and acknowledge even the little things that he does, it will go a long way. When you uphold him by letting him know how thankful you are for how hard he works to provide for you and the family, it's like he just won the lottery; at least for a day.

Affirmation from you lets him know that his efforts are not in vain and that he has your support and appreciation. It is also a need that seems to be hard-wired inside of him. Without even knowing it intellectually, it appears that a man has this emotional need for affirmation.

The issue that we've found in many relationships gone wrong is that if he can't get that affirmation at home, he naturally drifts elsewhere to find it. I use the word naturally here because it appears to be a natural inclination for a man to so desire words of affirmation that he is actually willing to risk doing the wrong thing in order to find them. When a man is affirmed by his spouse, he is more than a mere mortal. He is somehow transformed into a super-husband. He can leap tall buildings in a single bound; it's a bird, it's a plane, no it's super-husband that is just being affirmed by his wife.

I believe this is a part of the mystery the Bible refers to. The two shall become one. When a husband consistently gets that affirmation from his wife, he begins to crave it and he wants so much to please her. This is a powerful tool in the hands of a Godly woman that will lead to years and years of not only success in your relationships, but it will trickle over into every area of your life.

Sex

Just like we said earlier that romance does not mean sex for a woman; it is equally as important here to mention that romance does mean sex to most men. He desires sex, pure and simple.

While this is truly a hard-wired desire for most men, we are seeing in some cases where the woman has this desire even more so than the man. While I am not sure of all the reasons why, please be aware that this could very well be the case in your relationship and if so, don't think you're the only ones. The answer is still the same. Communicate, communicate, communicate and then come to agreement.

Talk about ways to meet this need while understanding balance is required in all things. Balance is a way of making sure we don't go too far to the left or too far to the right. Balance requires a great deal of both self-discipline as well as genuine care for one another. As we continue to communicate our desires to one another in a spirit of self-discipline and genuine care for one another, sex becomes both fulfilling to the man and at the same time takes away the drudgery from the woman. It becomes what I believe God intended for it to be. A plum pleasing pleasure!

Ω

What Every Woman Needs to Hear, What Every Man Needs to Know

Questions for Couple or Group Discussion

1. In what areas of our relationship have we experienced a lack of trust that lead to disappointment in each other?

2. How will we redefine our relationship in that area in order to defend against "the threat"?

3. Discuss the "Four Inward Needs of A Woman." Which need would I like to see my covenant partner focus more on? How would that make me feel?

4. Discuss "The Three Primary Needs of Men." Which need would I like to see my covenant partner focus more on? How would that make me feel?

-9-

Living in "The Blessing"
Covenant Relationship Law #4

God honors and blesses those who honor and bless the covenant relationship.

Below is a letter that expresses perfectly what this law is all about. It was written by a loving husband to his wife on the occasion of their 25th wedding anniversary.

"Wow! It's been 25 years!

I can honestly say that I love you more today than I ever have. You have taught me so much and I thank God for you daily. Before God created you in your mother's womb, He knew that we would be together. He made you in such a way as to make me better, with you, than I could ever be without you. I know that it's hard for some to believe and that's why I believe the bible refers to it as a mystery. "The two shall become one." We made it baby girl! We are ONE.

You taught me how precious your virginity was to you.

You taught me to value people and relationships over stuff and things.

You encouraged me to be the best that I could be at all times.

You allowed me to live my dream, even when my dreams were so big that others doubted and even laughed at me.

You have given birth to (2) of my beautiful daughters and have treated my oldest daughter with great kindness, grace and mercy. You also made sure I got the son I always wanted.

You have become a First Lady because God called me into full time ministry. Although we both have gone through a lot and have wanted to quit many times, your faith in God has NEVER failed. You see the God in me!

You have taught me how to love and serve without expecting anything in return; in fact, EXPECTING NOTHING IN RETURN.

You have taught me that people are human and they make mistakes in words and deeds; BUT deep in their heart-of-hearts, people are good. God is good and we were made in His image.

You made me believe that I was good even though I had so many mistakes in life.

I believe now! I will be OK. You won't have to work so hard for the next (25) years.

Enjoy the fruits of your labor. Look around! You have been a blessing to so many people.

I am honored that you call me your husband.

I love you Dee Henley and you will forever be my baby girl!"

God truly does honor and bless those who honor and bless the covenant relationship. We are told that a tree is known by the fruit that it bears and it works the same in relationships. A relationship is known by the fruit that it bears.

One way to know if you are being blessed in your relationship is to check the fruit. The fruit of a blessed relationship is love, joy, peace, patience, kindness, goodness, faithfulness, gentleness and self-control. After 25 years of marriage, I can honestly tell you that we've gone through a lot and have not always borne the fruit that we are bearing today. However, I can also attest to the fact that these simple covenant laws work. If you will apply them, they will also work in your relationship and you too will be fruit bearers. The two of you will become ONE.

The mystery of marriage for me was all about how the two become one. In other words, the mystery of marriage is all about creating ONENESS.

ONENESS

98

Vision is probably one of the most over-utilized words in our society today. It has been used for everything from selling cars to dish detergent. Every new CEO has to cast a vision of where the company is headed. A new head coach uses the word in order to forecast a vision of what the team will look like in three years. It basically gives them at least three years to turn a bad situation around or find another job.

Vision has been used as a metaphor that conjures up a dream like atmosphere that allows us to "see" the future of a thing, whatever that thing might be. Vision is the word that some people use when they have a dream that is so big the only way they can describe it and not look like a laughing stock is to call it a vision.

Vision has been used to give hope to the hopeless, a dream to the dreamless and to add fuel to the fire for those folks whose tanks have started to run dry. But what is vision and how does it really work? What is so significant about vision and why is clarity of vision so important? How do you take vision from being just another set of words used to manipulate the masses into something that is truly bigger than life itself? How do we use vision to bring life to a seemingly dead situation? These are questions we must all grapple with in order to take vision from just being words on a page to something that has the power to transform lives, relationships and ultimately the world, as we know it today.

Clarity of vision has a way of creating "oneness" like nothing else I have ever seen. Whether it's in ministry, business, sports or relationships, there is a power released in the atmosphere that creates a force that is virtually unstoppable.

Abraham got clarity of vision when God told him to go outside and look at the stars. God wanted to put an image or a vision in Abraham's mind that would constantly remind him of the promise that God had made to him. God told Abraham that he would have a son in his old age and not only that but he would have so many descendants that they would outnumber the stars. Once Abraham got that vision in his mind, he became unstoppable. Just like Abraham needed a vision, relationships need vision too. One Word from God will change your whole life.

In Proverbs 29:18, we read:

> Where there is no vision, the people
> perish: But he that keepeth the law,
> happy is he.

Where there is no vision, relationships began to die. I mean this both in a figurative and in a literal sense. Where couples or covenant partners have no vision, they perish. But for those that keep the Four Laws of Covenant Relationships, happy are they.

When couples begin to dream together, they began to grow together. When they have couple goals in addition to their individual goals, they begin to walk together. The Bible tells us plainly that it will be very tough to walk together unless we are in agreement.

> Can two walk together, unless they
> are agreed?
> -Amos 3:3

I am reminded of another ancient and very timeless story about a group of people that set out to build a building that would be so tall that it would reach the heavens. The following is an excerpt from that story which can be found in Genesis 11:1-9.

"At one time, the whole Earth spoke the same language. It so happened that as they moved out of the east they came upon a plain in the land of Shinar and settled down. They said to one another, "Come, let's make bricks and fire them well." They used brick for stone and tar for mortar.

Then they said, "Come, let's build ourselves a city and a tower that reaches Heaven. Let's make ourselves famous so we won't be scattered here and there across the Earth." God came down to look over the city and the tower those people had built. God took one look and said, "One people, one language; why, this is only a first step. No telling what they'll come up with next—they'll stop at nothing! Come, we'll go down and garble their speech so they won't understand each other." Then God scattered them from there all over the world. And they had to quit building the city. That's how it came to be called Babel, because there God turned their language into "babble." From there God scattered them all over the world."

Relationships work in a similar way. When men and women; or a husband and wife speak the same language and they stand in agreement, they can accomplish just about anything they put they mind to. It is my belief that both success and failure leaves clues. We have much to learn from both our successes in life as well as from our failures. This ancient story gives us lots of clues about clarity of vision.

First of all, it tells us the "main thing" is to check with God first, before we start to build. Before we start to build a relationship, we also should first check with God. We should ask questions like, "is this the right person for me?" or "are we equally yoked?" Checking with God before we build is critical and is definitely the "main thing."

We should always keep the "main thing"... the "main thing." I can't tell you the number of times we have missed God by not checking with Him first. We have so often, as a couple, had great plans only to find ourselves asking God to bless our plans versus saying to God, "thanks for the plan."

Just like Abraham got his vision from God, we too should seek to get our vision from God. Successful relationships begin with a vision from God. You won't have to ever wonder if you made the right choice, because you will know that you sought God before you started to build.

While the builders in our story failed to check with God prior to building, the story still gives us some keen insight on what makes up the successful chemistry of a vision that is caught by ALL the people. Some specifics are:

1. **Get on the same page.** *They all spoke the same language* or in other words they were all on the same page. In relationships, it is important to constantly stop and assess where we are in an effort to make sure we are on the same page.

2. **Move in the same direction.** *They all were moving east* or in other words they were all going in the same direction. When relationships are really on track, they are flowing in the same direction. Even if they make a wrong turn, they can work to fix it together and in the process share a

learning/growing experience. Unity is so critical to successful relationships.

3. **It is what it is.** *They settled on a plain* or in other words they settled on a spot that agreed with the environment. It would be tough to build such a mammoth structure on anything other than a plain. Sometimes covenant partners can share the exact same experience and both call it something different. One could be an optimist and the other a pessimist, but at some point they have to agree that it is what it is. Once they can agree on that, is when they can then make a decision to do something about it, but typically that only happens after a reality check has taken place.

4. **But, it doesn't have to always be this way.** They said to one another, "Come, let's make bricks and fire them well. They used brick for stone and tar for mortar." In other words they did something about their situation by communicating well and coming to agreement on the specifics or the "details" quickly. In a similar way, the relationships that we've found to be the most successful are the ones that know their situation or circumstance is never hopeless. They have the power to come into agreement and change their situation. They know just because it is what it is, doesn't mean that it always has to be that way. It is always within our ability to change our situation. With God, ALL things are possible!

They had just about all the ingredients of clarity of vision we have found that make up winning relationships. They knew what the vision was and they were very focused on getting it accomplished. They were moving in the same direction and I can tell you, by personal experience, great vision is very fluid and full of life. It is not static and lifeless or it will die.

They also understood the concept of "it is what it is" so they picked a spot to build (the plain) that was realistic from an environmental standpoint. I can't tell you the number of times that people have come to us with vision that just didn't line up with their environment. You know what I mean, the person that wants to borrow a million dollars to start a business and they have never even taken the time to write a business plan, study the target market or even look at the demographics of the area. In other words, they don't know if the environment is agreeable to the vision.

It works the same in relationships. You know the young couple that appear to be so in love and they want desperately to get married, but neither one of them have a job and they are both still in school. The vision just doesn't line up with their environment.

The Bible says, "If a man will not work, then he shouldn't eat." Well if he's not working and eating, he surely shouldn't be getting married. So many people wish that their environment was different and somehow believe that by wishing for it everything will turn out ok. That's just not the reality. This is what's known as make believe or just plain old-fashioned wishful thinking. We must understand that it is what it is and wishing it were different doesn't make it so.

Not only did they speak the same language, move in the same direction and find the right environment to build on, but they also communicated well and found a way to agree on the specifics or the "details." They understood that although it is what it is, it doesn't have to always be this way. We can do something about it. We have the power to change our situation.

To be more specific here, I would like to suggest that if you have an anger management problem, you can change your situation. Seek some help because there are lots of great anger management programs. Take a personality assessment and understand that while we can't change one another, we can learn how to work "best" with what we have.

If your finances are in need of help. You have the power to change your destiny. There are some great programs available from folks like Dave Ramsey and Crown Financial Ministry. My personal favorite is Crown Financial and the can be found at the website www.crown.org.

If you need a job, seek and find one. Start with what's available, do your best and then believe God for more. He said when we are faithful with a little, He can give us more. If you have problems with communication or conflict resolution, practice the exercises found throughout this book and answer the questions at the end of each chapter. If you need outside counsel, go to the Life

Innovations website at prepare-enrich.com or visit Dedan Ministry to Marriages website at dedan.org. There you can find a marriage mentor in your area that has been trained to help in those areas as well as many other relationship areas. Seek and you will find a Marriage Mentor that will work with you to find the help you seek.

The list of available resources goes on and on. If you seek help, you will find help and whether we know it or not, all of these issues, if not confronted, will eventually affect your relationships.

So many times great vision is bogged down with insignificant details or the time it takes to agree on little things. The little things have a way of taking care of themselves or they seem to just disappear. Remember to stay focused on the big picture and keep pushing through to the vision.

The only piece of the puzzle they missed was remembering to keep the "main thing"…the "main thing."

True Vision Comes From God

True vision comes from God and God alone.

"You have a God-sized vision so don't quit!"

Those are the words that I heard early one morning, prior to having sinus surgery. Those words have truly blessed my soul. I would be going under the knife in less than six hours to remove some polyps (a projecting growth or tumor in my nose as a result of having acute sinusitis). God was reminding me that I still had vision in me and there was no way I would die as long as I didn't quit. A vision gives life, hope and direction; and a God-sized vision gives lots of life.

Vision comes from God. When we have a right relationship with God, vision is automatic. Jesus reminded us of some very powerful words in Mark 4:12; "…they may be ever seeing but never perceiving, and ever hearing, but never understanding; otherwise they might turn and be forgiven!" Vision comes when we turn to God and get into a right relationship with him. "How?" you might ask. It starts with accepting Jesus, Christ as your personal Lord and Savior. However, it has to be an all or nothing deal. We can't just accept Jesus as our Savior, but we must also make Him the Lord of our life. As we do so, our relationship both to God and to one another becomes a Right-Relationship.

The world and society are quick to tell us that our marriage is not going to make it. In fact they quote statistics from the United States Bureau of the Census which say there are 2.3 million marriages in the United States every year and 1.2 million divorces. The average marriage lasted less than seven years and nearly two out of ten marriages ended before the third anniversary.

We are also told there has been a 1200% increase in the cohabitation rate over the past four decades and trends indicate that couples who cohabit prior to marriage have lower relationship satisfaction and an increased risk of divorce.

Studies also indicate a significant proportion of married couples experience serious marital conflict early in their relationships and very few engaged couples successfully anticipate the conflicts they will encounter in their marital relationships. And lastly, studies tell us that many couples do not have the communication skills necessary to resolve these conflicts.

The good news for us is that we get to decide. That's right, we decide. We have been told that the journey of a thousand miles starts with the first step. In truth, the journey of a thousand miles starts with a decision to take the journey. You have made the decision to not become a statistic because you have invested in this book. You have invested your time and attention and now you have made it to the end. But remember the end is really just the beginning. Now we have to do the work of actually living it out. If you are willing to make the decision to do what you've learned in this book, I look forward to seeing you at the finish line. Because in the end – we win!

Ω

What Every Woman Needs to Hear,
What Every Man Needs to Know

Questions for Couple Discussion

After praying and asking for God's guidance answer the following questions together:

1. Where are we now as a couple?

2. Where would we like to be as a couple?

3. How are we going to get there together?

Questions for Annual Goal Setting

After praying and asking for God's guidance answer the following questions together:

1. What were our most memorable accomplishments over the last year?

2. What are two or three things we would like to do over the next year?

3. What would we like to accomplish this year in school, work or our relationship?

4. What is the one thing about myself that I would like to improve this year?

5. What would be the most fun thing for us to do this year?

6. What will we do to help/serve someone outside our family?
7. How will we grow closer to God this year?
8. How much would we like to save?

A Final Prayer

It's only once we understand the purpose of the Creator and not the purposes of the creation that we will truly live out our purpose. Help us to know your purpose Father... in Christ's name.

Amen.

CPSIA information can be obtained
at www.ICGtesting.com
Printed in the USA
LVHW080425011022
729703LV00005B/14